ADOBE® MASTER CLASS
PHOTOSHOP®

INSPIRING ARTWORK AND TUTORIALS BY ESTABLISHED AND EMERGING ARTISTS

ADOBE
PRESS

Adobe

ADOBE® MASTER CLASS: PHOTOSHOP®
Inspiring artwork and tutorials by established and emerging artists
Curated by Ibarionex Perello

This Adobe Press book is published by Peachpit, a division of Pearson Education.

For the latest on Adobe Press books, go to
www.adobepress.com
To report errors, please send a note to errata@peachpit.com.

Acquisitions, Project, and Developmental Editor: Rebecca Gulick
Cover Design: Charlene Charles-Will
Interior Design: Charlene Charles-Will and Kim Scott, Bumpy Design
Compositing: Charlene Charles-Will and Danielle Foster
Copy Editor: Patricia J. Pane
Production Coordinator: Becky Winter
Cover Images: Miss Aniela, Jim Kazanjian, Ibarionex Perello, James Porto, Martine Roch,
Tim Tadder, Sean Teegarden, Dean West

ISBN-13: 978-0-321-89048-1
ISBN-10:   0-321-89048-5

9 8 7 6 5 4 3 2 1
Printed and bound in the United States of America

FOREWORD

Those who tell the stories rule the world.

Storytelling through images is what makes us human. From the cave paintings of our most remote ancestors and throughout the entire history of art to our days, images are the shortest path to another fellow human's emotions. We humans make marks before we can speak or write. Our need to share feelings found its best outlet through visual communication.

The great variety of images presented in this book are a beautiful collection of stories told and of feelings shared.

I have been a Photoshop user from the very beginning, when the first version hit the market in 1990. From that very beginning—and I was still a student at the Art Center College of Design then—I mused over the power of that devilish pixel-moving application. I lost sleep over it, and spent countless hours in the newly equipped computer labs. Even my teachers thought I was exaggerating. I felt the power. I felt that things were about to change, and this inspired me to experiment extensively. Indeed, image manipulation had come to the masses, and it changed the way we create images, for whichever media, from print to video. This was the beginning of an entirely new storytelling era.

Photoshop has become part of our popular culture as the tool that lets people "modify" images, be that for good or bad, be it subtle or bold. In any case, it changed our perception entirely. Furthermore, with the advent of digital cameras and the democratization of photography, the process of image manipulation has become even speedier, allowing artists to experiment faster and become more spontaneous, removing the time-consuming and costly developing and scanning processes.

As a Worldwide Evangelist at Adobe, I have the great fortune to meet creative professionals from all over the globe, each with her or his own way of creating imagery, and it is truly humbling to see how the software we create is being used in the most unexpected ways. One of the benefits here is that, unlike traditional painting, digital artists can move, change their mind, cancel, or add on the electronic canvas at will, freeing up the creative process all the way to the intended purpose of the artwork.

Today, Photoshop has become an incredibly powerful, industry-leading compositing and imaging tool, allowing artists to realize their visions and share them with the rest of us in ways that were unthinkable only a few decades ago. The 31 artists featured in this book are a great example of this. Not only do we get to look at their visions, but we are also taught about how they created their images. Sharing knowledge and art. It does not get better than that.

—Rufus Deuchler
 Senior Worldwide Evangelist,
 Creative Cloud, Adobe

ADOBE MASTER CLASS **PHOTOSHOP**

INTRODUCTION

For some, photography is a document, a print, or a collection of pixels that helps to spur a memory or confirm the details of an event or occurrence. For others, photography is about the tools and devices used to create them. It can also be an endless source of visual noise that bombards us every time we launch a web browser, open up a magazine, or simply walk down a street littered with advertisements.

But for the artists in this book, photography is more than that. It's a unique means of expression that allows each to express an idea, a feeling, and a moment within fractions of a second. Unlike a play or motion picture that may demand several hours of our time or a book that may consume days or weeks, an image has to attract and hold our attention in seconds. It hopefully connects and seduces the viewer to linger for a little longer and take in all that the artist has to offer.

In today's digital world, the tens of thousand of images that pass in our view do not even register long enough to be distractions, making it all the more challenging for any person practicing the art of the photographic image.

The artists in this book have taken on this challenge, each in her or his own very unique way. Though each uses similar photographic tools, including Adobe Photoshop, the value of their work doesn't lie in model of camera or some digital workflow, but how they used those tools to successfully traverse the empty space between imagination and art.

Photoshop as a tool has transformed the process of photography, creating opportunities to explore, to experiment, and to revolutionize how we create and see photography. Whether it's in the hands of portraitists like Sean Teegarden or William George Wadman or conceptualists such as Richard Baxter and Martine Roche, software becomes as much of an extension of the eye and the hand as the camera itself ever was.

It provides people like Gediminas Pranckevičius and Jim Kazanjian and Maki Kawakita the chance to create completely new worlds that, despite their hyperreality, still keep us tethered to our own imperfect world.

Photographers can use this tool to challenge our view of history and truth, such as in the work of Stephen Marc and Christopher Schneberger.

Each artist in his or her own way has not merely created a piece of beauty, but is also challenging us to see the world in a different way. It becomes an invitation to gaze upon each other and the world that we share from someone else's perspective. Sometimes that view can be based on the shared reality of nature, as with Tony Sweet, or that of the absurd and humorous with James Porto, but whichever the case, it's an invitation to discover that there is more than one way to see.

As these photographers share their work and their process with you in this book, I hope that it serves as a reminder that the power of photography lies in its ability to communicate and link us together. It reminds us of what we have in common, rather than what makes us separate and different.

There is a lot of joy in the creation and the viewing of these works, and if this book spurs you even a small way to take advantage of it, it will have succeeded.

—Ibarionex Perello
   November 2012

ADOBE® MASTER CLASS

PHOTOSHOP®

Adam Baron

"This is the world I want to live in, with all its unattainable shiny perfection."

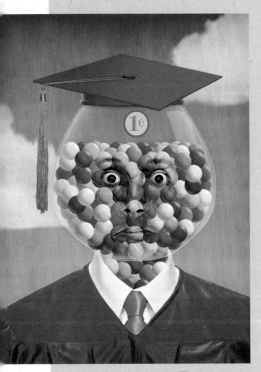

PENNY FOR YOUR THOUGHTS, 2011

For as long as I can remember, I have always been fascinated with the perfect world as portrayed by illustrators in print ads and magazines from the midcentury: the dapper, genial, fedora-wearing father coming home from a hard day's work at the office; the beautiful, elegant mother wearing an apron over her dress as she bakes cookies; little Johnny painting his model airplane and little Suzy combing her dolly's hair. This is a world of white picket fences, milkmen, cars with stylish curves and lines, and friendly police officers. It's a world where a pretty stewardess took your order for your double martini while you reclined in your comfortable airline seat as you flew first class to Hawaii.

To what degree this world ever really existed I'll never know. I was simply born too late to experience it firsthand. What I know of it existed solely on paper, impeccably rendered by an artist, no doubt hired to convey that perfection to sell a product or service. But this is the world I want to live in, with all its unattainable shiny perfection.

A large part of my work is trying to reconcile my vision of this perfect world of the past with the realities of today's world. The man in the hat, a recurring figure in my work, represents that 50's prototypical everyman thrust into the problems of real life—and maybe not coping with it so well. In my work, he is placed in scenarios where he is overworked, isolated, stressed, marginalized, or constantly reminded about his own mortality. And like all the action figures we abused and tortured as children, I toy with him only because I love him so much.

AUTUMN YEARS, 2008

He Has Left Us Alone, 2010

HE HAS LEFT US ALONE
BUT SHAFTS OF LIGHT
SOMETIMES GRACE
THE CORNER OF OUR ROOMS

The War with Myself, 2012

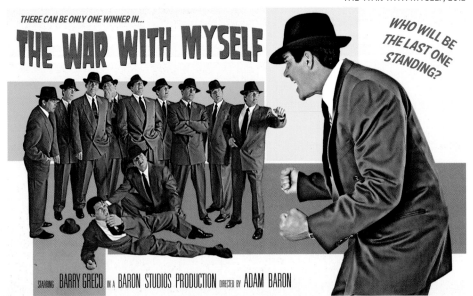

THERE CAN BE ONLY ONE WINNER IN...

THE WAR WITH MYSELF

WHO WILL BE THE LAST ONE STANDING?

STARRING BARRY GRECO IN A BARON STUDIOS PRODUCTION DIRECTED BY ADAM BARON

LIKE NIGHT AND DAY, 2007

Creating a Winged Vision

In my piece *There, There*, I had the idea that the man in the hat, a recurring figure in my work, is looking rather distraught. While contemplating his woes, a host of butter-flies are perching upon him, and despite looking pretty, they offer him little consola-tion and perhaps only serve to make him look more ridiculous.

❶ Starting with an HDR Shot

I started this image by taking a five-exposure HDR (high dynamic range) photo of myself. I processed the image in an HDR program called Photomatix, from HDRsoft. The settings I used produced a result that looked like an illustration, but it's still quite rough.

② Creatively Using Unsharp Mask

I then isolated the image from the background and adjusted the colors and contrast. I used the color replacement brush to produce uniform coloring and clean up the variations of the HDR image. I employed one of my favorite tools, Unsharp Mask, set to very high values (a radius of around 45 pixels) to create an illustrated look. This technique produces exaggerated contrasts, which resemble the look of commercial illustration from the 50s. Finally, I used the Topaz Adjust plug-in from Topaz Labs to smooth out the image and eliminate unwanted noise and details.

③ Picking a Sky

I wanted a sky background and remembered an HDR set I had done at Vizcaya Museum and Gardens in Miami. I found an appropriate photo and cropped it to just the sky. I then imported that into my main picture as a layer.

4 **Placement**

I then placed the man I had previously isolated into that sky image on a separate layer. Because the man was already isolated, the sky on the lower layer showed through. I then enabled the grid view to allow me to use principles such as the rule of thirds to improve the composition.

5 **Combining Layers**

Once I have a few main elements in a picture, I start titling the file as a mock-up and save incremental changes, adding a version number after "mock-up." This way, if I notice a mistake, I simply go back to a previous version and swap something out.

6 Photographing Elements

While I had a few butterfly shots already in my arsenal, I needed many more variations to make the shot interesting, so I paid a visit to Butterfly World in Coconut Creek, Florida, and shot the images I needed, including this one taken through the glass of a display case.

7 Isolating Butterfly Parts

After a very time-consuming process of isolating the many butterfly shots I had taken, I created a "butterfly parts department" where I could assemble them with different wings and bodies. The heads and bodies are from photos, and I drew the antennae and legs in Photoshop.

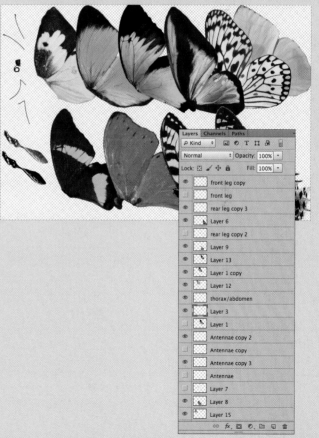

8 Assembling More Butterflies

I then assembled the butterflies from the separate pieces and copied them over to the main image.

9 Adding Drop Shadows

I began placing the butterflies and adding drop shadows where appropriate. I did this by first duplicating the layer of the butterfly, bringing up the Hue/Saturation, and sliding the "lightness" slider all the way to black to create a silhouette of the butterfly. I then moved that layer behind the butterfly and manually positioned it to where I thought the shadow should be. I erased parts of the shadow with the eraser brush where needed. Finally, I adjusted the opacity of the shadow layer so it wasn't completely black and the man's jacket could still be seen through the shadow.

⑩ Sharpening

Applying some degree of output sharpening is important whether the image is destined for a computer screen or paper. It's important for printing, as different types of paper will respond differently and require different amounts of sharpening to produce a good final look.

Conclusion

This is the final composition I decided on—all the butterflies and their shadows are in place. I then added a texture on top of the whole image, set to Overlay mode, which gives it a slight vignetting and adds an oil painting quality to the image.

Holger Maass

"Our photographs are trying to tell stories in a single picture."

ABSOLUT SWEDEN

The work of Holger Maass and his team is a mixture of real sets and digital postproduction. Very often real sets are built in the studio, which sometimes takes weeks of planning and preparation. For the shooting with German celebrity Barbara Schöneberger, a team of 10 people, including specialists from the TV and movie industries, helped to set up the scene. In many cases, even the fashion is specially designed for the shoot. Even when they try to make it real, there is still a lot of postproduction to support the statement and the idea behind the photographs.

Our photographs are trying to tell stories in a single picture. Some of the stories are historical or from Greek mythology, such as "Leda with the Swan" and "Judith and Holofernes." For both of those shoots we studied the old masters like Caravaggio, Rembrandt, and Dürer before creating our own versions. Other stories are inspired and influenced by actual media and events of modern day.

ANGRIFF DER KILLERKRABBE

ELM-ELMN

You Can´t Beat The Feeling

Cowgirl

▶ Barbara Schöneberger

Tim Tadder

"I have always been a little outside the box when it comes to creating art."

WATERHATS 1, 2012

I create images that are different. This is not by pure intent; it's just my way of seeing. I have always been a little outside the box when it comes to creating art. I always take on a greater challenge than the norm. I try to make images that are bigger, better, more complex, and more interesting than those around me. For me, it's not enough to create work that is good. I risk and try for great. Sometimes that means failing, but when it works, I get an image that is really strong and very compelling.

My images are very much a medium to communicate how I see the world around me as well as the people I relate to. I love shooting powerful and intense people, and so, naturally, athletes tend to be the most common subjects that work with me. I also love color and the intensity color can bring to images. Much of my work has a color tone and saturation that is very identifiable, which is again just a way I see. For me, it's the thing that makes my images feel complete.

I am highly motivated when I focus on a new image concept, and nothing stands in my way of creating a new vision. The ideas come during the quiet stretches between creative outbursts, when my need to express something new motivates me from thinking about it to actually doing it. Creating something new quiets my active mind and actually gives me a great sense of peace. But soon enough, the restlessness returns and I need to once again go through the cycle. So I guess you could say I make art to satisfy an inner drive to create. As technology opens up more creative possibilities, I intend on using it to make even more exciting imagery.

▶ CORDURA CLIMBER, 2008

Doordie Poster, 2010

Fishtank 2, 2012

Waterhats 2, 2012

UNTITLED, 2008

CALL OF JUAREZ, 2009

Jaclyn Corrado

"I am never looking to create the 'perfect image.' I enjoy producing pieces that appear destructed and manipulated."

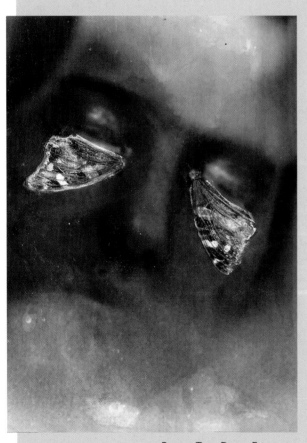

People That Don't Exist, 2012

As a young artist, I realize I am still experimenting, and I will most likely continue to do so for the remainder of my career. I am constantly changing the way I produce work, sometimes making collages, using only digital media at other times, or going the analog route and using film. I am never looking to create the "perfect image." I enjoy producing pieces that appear destructed and manipulated. When approaching an image, I am inclined to base the entire shoot around an outfit or color scheme. I spend hours on weekends rummaging through thrift shops and flea markets for garments that inspire my work. At this moment in time, my images are most often inspired by a general idea rather than a story line.

I'm still very new to photography and know there is always more to learn. Photoshop is a major contributor to my photography and I know its constant innovations will always allow me to experiment and grow. My goal is to incorporate my art into the world of fashion, so it's important to have my own style, one that can be associated with several different genres of photography. Most of all, I want my work, regardless of what it is being used for, to be recognizable no matter what genre I choose to pursue. (Author photo by Raymond Colon.)

▶ Identical Divers, 2012

GARDENER 2, 2012

BRITTA AND BRITTANY, 2012

1973, 2012

STAMP, 2012

Scott Stulberg

"My photographs let my imagination come to life."

I've had many gifts in my life, but maybe the best one of all was the camera my father gave me when I was 10 years old. Albert Einstein said, "Imagination is more important than knowledge," and with that camera, my photographs let my imagination come to life. A few years later, a whole new world opened up for me when my parents built a darkroom for me in our basement. Under the safelights, smelling chemicals, and listening to music, I lost all track of time watching my images come to life. Although I've been using Photoshop for many years, it was the countless hours in the darkroom that made me fall in love with photography.

I feel just like Cartier-Bresson felt, that the camera is an extension of my eye. And although a photograph is seen with the eye, it is made with the mind. And my mind always seems to be surveying the constant movement as life unfolds, because great moments are born from great opportunity. Capturing that moment in time keeps us living that moment forever.

I love shooting so many different things at home and abroad, and though I haven't shot film in years, I realize that photography is more than talking about pixels. It is about vision, ideas, and the willingness to allow your imagination to soar.

UNTITLED 1, 2008

Untitled 2, 2011

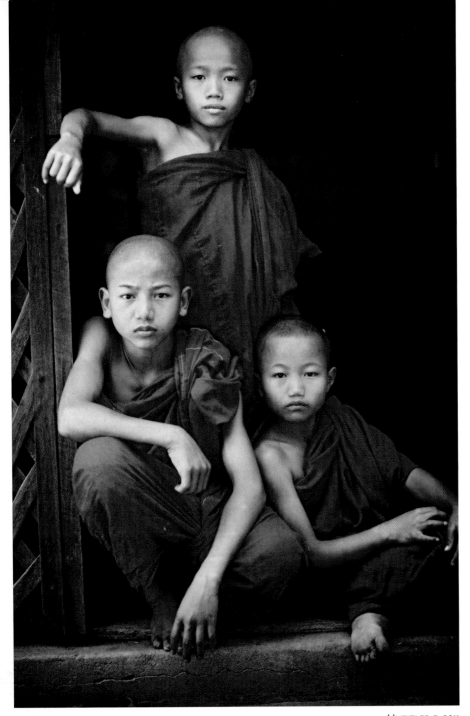

UNTITLED 3, 2011

Untitled 4, 2007

Untitled 5, 2012

Untitled 6, 2011

Creating a Different Look with Blending Modes

One of my favorite ways to work on my photos is to convert them to black-and-white first and then use blending modes when I bring them back into color. This is such an easy technique, but the differences between the before and after can be pretty spectacular. I use this technique for so many different kinds of images that vary in many ways, from travel photography to landscapes and of course for portraits.

❶ Setting Up the Shot

When shooting this image of a young monk I met in Burma, I pulled the boy's robe onto his head and placed him exactly where I wanted him by his monastery. The light was good, and I had him look straight at me and try to show no emotion. I knew I would have exactly what I wanted and had the basis for a great conversion later in Photoshop.

2 Converting to Black-and-White

I then opened the image in Nik Silver Efex Pro2, my favorite black-and-white conversion software. After working in the darkroom for over 20 years, I'm very spoiled when it comes to creating a very realistic black-and-white or sepia-toned look in Photoshop. Although I am converting it to black-and-white, I know that my final outcome is going to be in color.

3 Using Presets

I used the default preset as my basis. Though the software provides a diverse range of looks, I prefer to start with as neutral a look as possible to suit my particular vision and taste.

4 **Customizing B&W**

I then used all of my sliders and controls on the right side of the plug-in to give me the exact black-and-white look that I was looking for. It gave me just what I wanted, and then I hit OK and it brought into Photoshop on its own layer.

5 **Fine-tuning the Conversion**

Because the blending mode's default is Normal, the black-and-white version of the image blocks the view to the original layer. This is fine if all I want is a black-and-white image, but I want something more.

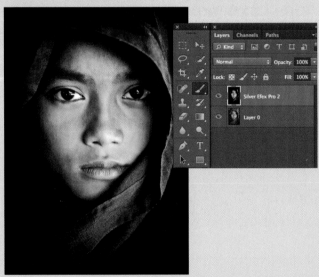

6 Choosing a Blending Mode

My next step was easy, as all I did was to start playing with my blending modes on the black-and-white layer to see which look might be the best. Blending modes are one of the easiest ways to totally change an image in Photoshop. You choose a blend mode, and then see how it interacts with your particular image; every image reacts differently. I played with quite a few different ones and then realized that Hard Light gave me just what I was looking for. It was still a little bit strong, but that was because the opacity was 100%.

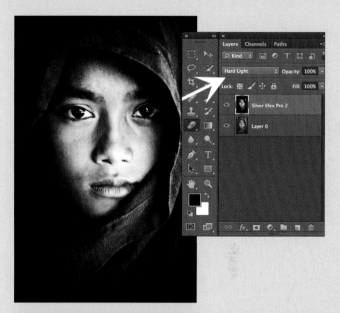

7 Adjusting the Opacity

All I had to do now was lower the opacity of the black-and-white layer and get it close to how I wanted it to look at the end. I lowered the opacity of the layer to 68%. Because the effect was a little too strong on the face, I used a layer mask, and with a brush at about 25% capacity, I brushed out some of the harsh look to go back to the original feel and color.

8 **Using Photoshop's Layer Mask**

I used the layer mask in Photoshop to soften his face.

9 **Getting the Soft Look on the Face**

You can now see that his face is a little bit softer. There is nothing as important as mastering layer masks in Photoshop to give you exactly what you envision!

Conclusion

The final image is completely different from the original. However, it is exactly what I hoped to get when I originally photographed my little buddy that special day in Burma. Blending modes are one of the best ways to make your images take on a whole new life, and the sky is the limit when it comes to using blending modes in Photoshop.

Alexander Corvus

"These ideas are generally absurd, and they are unclear to me until everything is completed."

The fundamental principle of my art is usually born from an idea that I ruminate on for a long period of time. However, the final photograph is often unrecognizable from those original ideas. Those ideas continue their mutation during a photo session and subsequent image processing. Everything begins from the idea that grows into sketches, and then production starts. Ideas of such projects arise spontaneously, having jumped out from the depth of my subconsciousness, from any phrase from a book, a piece of music, a picture. These ideas are generally absurd, and they are unclear to me until everything is completed.

I try to draw a few ideas from the works of other photographers, artists, or cinema. Fresh visual impressions have a habit of suppressing an imagination's freedom. My latest projects were inspired by an attempt to make a start from widespread film images, in which I explored apocalyptic ideas but through a filter of irony and absurdity.

UNTITLED 1, 2012

▶ UNTITLED 2, 2012

UNTITLED 3, 2012

Martine Roch

> "It's the combination of animal and human that creates my work. We are complementary in life, and so we are in my portraits."

THE GOOD FRIEND, 2011

▶ INSOMNIA, 2009

My work is based on my love for both animals and photography. It all started with the observation of animal expressions. Anybody can see that sometimes animals are almost like humans. And, of course, we all have an animal in us. I remember a friend of my grandfather looking just like his dog! They had the same walk, the same expressions, and even the same hairstyle. That was years ago, but I still remember them together walking down the street. So it's the combination of animal and human that creates my work. We are complementary in life, and so we are in my portraits.

The base of the image is one of the antique photographs that I have collected for years. These old photographs have a soul. I love the style of the costumes, the people's postures, and the décor, which is sometimes really gorgeous—I try to keep it as much as I can. The images are hand-coloured from sepia. I take the photos of the animals myself. My model is often Boudi, my faithful Labrador (who is now 14 years old). I see animals with love and respect, not with mockery.

When I make an image, I take time to get acquainted with the personage. So I imagine a little quote to go with the image, or only a name to give to the character. My primary goal with my work is to bring a smile to people's face. Then I leave the public to react however they feel when looking at the personages.

THE BOSS, 2012

THE FASHION VICTIM, 2011

THE ARISTOCRAT, 2011

THE EXPLORER, 2010

▶ GOOD BYE, 2009

Marcos López

> "Marcos López is an artist whose work reflects clear historical aspects of his country of Argentina."

Marcos López is an artist whose work reflects clear historical aspects of his country of Argentina. In several of his images, he depicts different places in the country related to his childhood, youth, and adulthood.

After the end of the country's dictatorship, López found himself immersed in a world that was being transformed by a new sense of freedom and living intensely. His influences also included Latin and American pop culture, both in terms of his use of color and iconography.

The result is a series of hand-colored photographs, conceived to express the wounds of the painful memories of his motherland. In his images, he strives to explore the tragedy of the human condition and the price of cruelty.

SUITE BOLIVARIANA, 2007

El Cumpleaños de la Directora, 2009

GAUCHO GIL, 2008

LUCHADOR ARENA MEX, 2008

COMIDA RÁPIDA, 2008

El Martir, 2005

Il Piccollo Vapore, 2007

William George Wadman

"I strive for control and vision, a slow-honed perfection, often composited together from multiple source images in post-production."

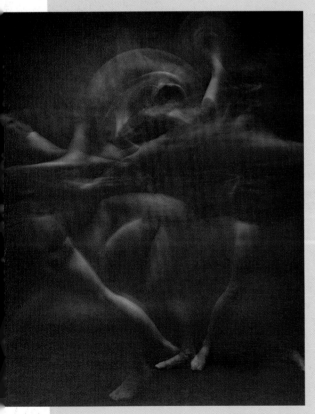

MOTION 26, 2010

I didn't start in the visual arts. In fact, I have a degree in music, and no training in illustration or painting. This is a bit ironic since I'm something of a classicist and a voracious autodidact who strives for my images to invoke the paintings of Caravaggio, Rembrandt, and Rockwell in the photographic domain. I want my images to reflect that level of craft—to be deliberate and intentional, and not just a lucky get. I strive for control and vision, a slow-honed perfection, often composited from multiple source images in post-production.

My conceptual portraits are previsualized with the intent to tell a story, to illustrate a moment, which needs to be imagined and expanded toward both the past and future in the mind of the viewer. They are a voyeuristic glimpse into someone else's world, sometimes fantastic or silly; other times scary or even sad, but always pivotal.

When a career as an art director in the advertising world proved unsatisfying, I decided in 2007 to change directions and swore that as a photographer, I would only create the kind of images that made me happy to look at. So that when I look back from my deathbed, I can view a body of work that is beautiful but honest, varied yet cohesive, and perhaps, timeless so that it may inspire, just as the work of others has done for me.

CynthiaSmith, 2009

MOTION 32, 2010

PARTY-564, 2011

DANGOTTESMAN, 2009

CHRISBERGER, 2009

Climbing the Walls

It all started with a vague idea of having my model, Gatlin, standing cool on a wall, as if he belonged there and it was no big deal. I set up my tripod and took some shots of this wall near a café in my Brooklyn neighborhood. I swapped lenses a bit to get it right, ending on my trusty 28mm prime. Always trying to imagine how a person might fit into the frame. Since I wasn't doing any scale shifting (making things smaller or larger than they are), it's best to use the same lens for each element of the shot. That way the perspective and any lens effects stay constant, making it easier to blend the two in the end. In fact, placing the person in the same place in the frame that they'll be in the final shot really helps, allowing you to overlay the two and just mask them in.

1 **Creating the Plate**

This image is right out of the camera and, as you can tell, pretty boring. In fact, it's not a very good picture at all. That said, there's more to it than just taking the shot. You've got to rotate your thinking a bit and remember that Gatlin's going to be projecting six feet from that wall, so make sure you allow enough room. I also measure from the camera to the plane where I think he's going to be, and the distance from the camera to the wall.

❷ Adjusting Contrast

The next step is adjusting the contrast. I add a Curves Adjustment layer and give it the traditional S curve to increase contrast by darkening the bottom half and brightening the highlights. Then I fill the layer's mask with black, which essentially turns it off for the whole image. That way I can use a paintbrush to draw in white where I want the effect to happen—in this case, mostly the wall Gatlin will be standing on. A little too contrasty at this point? Maybe, but this is fine for now.

❸ Photographing the Subject

Gatlin is very tall, a blessing because it gave me the idea of having him twisting to get his face in the same orientation as the viewer. To get the angles right, I use the measurements I took when shooting the plate. I set the camera-tripod to the same height as the distance the camera was from the wall outside. Then I mark a spot on the paper based on the distance from the camera where I imagined him standing. For the angle of the camera, I lined up the rightmost focus point in my camera with the spot on the wall where I imagined his feet would be. Then when I shot him I panned the camera down until that same focus point was on his feet. For lighting, I thought about how the light would fall on him in the final image—from the sky above, which is to his left in the picture. I used two umbrellas, a big one to his left to mimic the light and another camera left to fill in shadows.

4 Positioning the Subject

The next step is to copy Gatlin from his picture and paste him into a new layer over the background plate. Then I add a layer mask and begin filling that mask in with black to hide those areas. There are plenty of ways to do this using Magic Wand, Lasso, and Marquee tools to select different regions and fill them with black, or even by using a black paintbrush. I use all of the above, because different areas require different solutions. In the end, I'm often working at 100% with a very small brush to get it to blend just right. The advantage of using a mask instead of just erasing the area you don't want is that you can always go back and paint sections back in with white if you make a mistake.

⑤ Combining and Shadows

The overall perspective is pretty close, and he fits fine, but the color and contrast is a bit off, and the lack of shadows makes it very obviously faked. So the next step is to add some shadows below Gatlin. I wanted it to look like there was more than just the sun lighting him, maybe a softbox a few feet above the camera position. So the shadows are not right below, but also falling away behind him. On top of the big soft shadow, I need darker, harder ones under his feet anywhere the shoes would be lifted off a half-inch or so. I'm not constantly thinking about every setting and angle, but when you're doing artistic composites like this, it's being obsessive about those kinds of details that make the difference between silly and believable.

6 Shaping the Light

This image is close, but there's still a disconnect between the subject and the plate due to slightly mismatched lighting; the side of his body facing the ground should be more in shadow. So now I go in with more Curves Adjustment layers and masks to shape the light a bit more. With one Curves layer I pull the center point down a bit so that it darkens the whole picture. Then, like before, I fill its mask with black and use a white medium-soft paintbrush to paint in the shadow to darken the side of his body that's closest to the ground. With another Curves Adjustment layer I add some contrast to the rest of his body. Looks pretty good, but it's not quite finished.

❼ Applying a Vignette

The final thing I like to do is add some vignetting to make him pop off the background a bit. Again, there are a number of ways to do this. I use another Curves Adjustment layer pulled down to darken the whole thing. Then I select its layer mask again and use the elliptical Marquee tool to select a generous oval around Gatlin. I soften the selection by choosing Select > Modify > Feather with a radius of 250px. This gives me a puffy, soft selection around the subject, which I then fill with black. This effect focuses the viewers' attention on what I choose to highlight in the image. I also add a film grain using a stock medium-gray film-grain image that I paste into a new layer at the top of the stack. I set its blend mode to Overlay and opacity to 50%. The grain over the whole composite helps to blend elements together a bit more so it looks less like a composite.

Conclusion

So there you have it. Two pictures and a couple hours of obsession in Photoshop. As a general rule, I'm not a meticulous photographer. I'm not constantly thinking about every setting and angle, but when you're doing artistic composites like this, being obsessive about those kinds of details makes the difference between silly and believable.

Christopher Schneberger

> "With these narratives, I mean to entertain the viewer and immerse them in a story."

My work for the past decade has involved the supernatural and tropes of historical exhibition. The line between the two is made uncertain by supporting documents, both authentic and counterfeit, exhibited along with the work.

I have completed four such stories, each set in early 20th Century America. *The Strange Case of Dr. Addison and the Crosswell Twins* centers on a pair of twin sisters, one of whom has died mysteriously but appears to her surviving sibling in spirit form. Charles Addison, an amateur scientist and photographer attempting to disprove the spirit's presence, photographed them.

A Case of Levitation: The Story of Frances Naylor tells of a girl who lost her legs in infancy but later developed the ability to levitate. She wasn't allowed outside her home but was photographed by her father, who was fascinated by her gift.

Magic and Murder at the Candy Factory: The Story of Anna Sula involves an orphan girl who was murdered at the candy factory where she worked. Later, discovered photographs reveal that she had psychokinetic powers and was involved in séances that may have led to her demise.

I'm currently engaged in a new series of work, *Glimmer: The Haunting of the Graham House*, which involves a contemporary family living with the ghost of a girl from the early 1900s who visits them through reflections.

With these narratives, I mean to entertain the viewer and immerse them in a story. At the same time, I bring into question notions of history, factual accuracy, museums, and pseudoscience.

FRANNY AND GEORGE WALTZING, 2005

Frances with Pram, Front Porch, 2005

FRANCES DESCENDING THE STAIRS, 2005

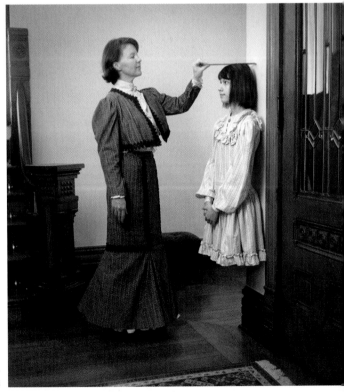

MEASURING FRANCES, 2005

SARAH AT THE PIANO, 2011

JOHN AT THE FIREPLACE, 2011

Stephen Marc

> "The work allows me to bring together and share materials from diverse places and to create relationships within the work that invite viewers to make discoveries...."

I am a photographer and digital montage artist who addresses the African Diaspora with an emphasis on the black experience within American history. My work is an interpretative view that features historical landscapes and architectural structures that are combined with period documents, illustrated newspapers, decorative and utilitarian objects, as well as pertinent modern references, including commemorative events and individuals of note.

My explorations range from the Underground Railroad and slavery to black pioneers with connections to the American West, and icons of collective Freedom Movement (Civil Rights and Black Power); to creative relocations of primarily pre-1935 black representations found in illustrated newspapers featuring documentary news accounts along with commercialized "Black Americana" stereotypes on postcards, trade cards, and collectable household objects.

The *Passage on the Underground Railroad* project (2000–2009) was created in order to describe individual UGRR sites inside and out. While researching and creating these interpretative views of the UGRR sites, I recognized a need to address the larger institution of slavery that defined that period. The resulting montages depict plantation quarters and crops, letters, legal documents, news source text and illustrations and such, to provide additional background information.

I am intrigued with how history is layered. I revisited parts of the country and discovered the complexity in the path individual lives took and the web of connections across distance and generations. The work allows me to bring together and share materials from diverse places and to create relationships within the work that invite viewers to make discoveries and come to terms with challenging issues regarding the cultural construct of black identity within American history.

UNTITLED 1

UNTITLED 2

UNTITLED 3

UNTITLED 4

UNTITLED 5

Untitled 6

Untitled 7

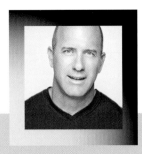

Joel Grimes

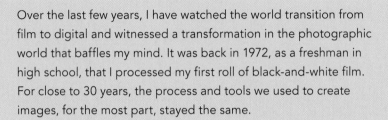

> "All the techniques, tools, and new-fangled processes are of absolutely no value without the creative mind."

Over the last few years, I have watched the world transition from film to digital and witnessed a transformation in the photographic world that baffles my mind. It was back in 1972, as a freshman in high school, that I processed my first roll of black-and-white film. For close to 30 years, the process and tools we used to create images, for the most part, stayed the same.

A few years ago, in the midst of the digital technological revolution, I sat down and asked myself a question. With all the new changes we were experiencing, what one variable has stayed the same? It hit me like a ton of bricks. Over the last 100-plus years the process and tools have constantly changed, but the one thing no technological advancement will ever encroach upon is the creative process. Yes, it takes an artist to create. All the techniques, tools, and new-fangled processes are of absolutely no value without the creative mind.

It is the creative mind that takes the tools at hand to generate a one-of-a-kind masterpiece, something that represents the very vision and soul of the artist. It is this amazing process that makes creating an image so much fun.

Today, it is possible to reach a million viewers in one day. Today, you can become a rock star overnight. All you need is a Flickr, Facebook, or Instagram and the world is at your fingertips. We are in the greatest age of photography since its conception, and in the end, it has everything to do with our desires as human beings to create. Technical proficiency at best can produce a boring image, but to be an artist and create, with a click of a button, you can win over millions of viewers.

NEW ORLEANS CHARTRES STREET, 2006

JESSICA
BACKGROUND
TREE ROOTS, 2011

DRE MERRIT
NEW ORLEANS
STREET LAMP, 2010

COUPLES AT BAR, 2011

KERRON-SEPOVIA DAM, 2009

SPECIAL FX, 2006

SAUL UA-STADIUM NIGHT, 2009

Enhancing the Light

When I saw this dapper fellow walking down the street, I knew that I had to make an image of him. After he agreed to be photographed, I positioned him so that I could use a bus shelter as the background. It was an overcast day and so the resulting light was ideal for making this portrait. Harsh, high-contrast light would have been an issue because of the darkness of his skin against the light-colored suit. It was that very contrast that I knew was the image's strength and its challenge.

1 Optimizing the Raw File

Because I knew that I was going to be pretty aggressive with the processing of this image, I adjusted my raw file to maintain as much shadow and highlight detail as possible. Though I tweaked the contrast with a slight levels adjustment, I made it a point not to be too aggressive at this early stage of my editing.

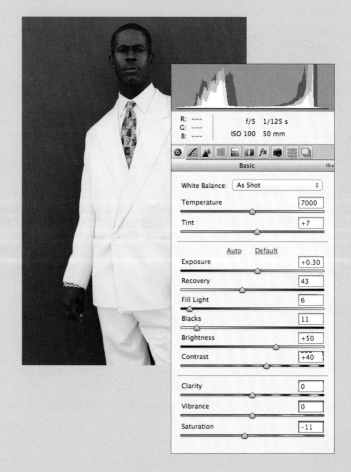

❷ Working the Suit

The biggest issue that I needed to contend with was the suit. Though the image was properly exposed, the details of the suit were skewing heavily to the brighter highlights. So, I made a selection using the Magic Wand tool. With the selection active, I created a Curves adjustment and brought down the overall exposure to pull out the detail and darken the suit.

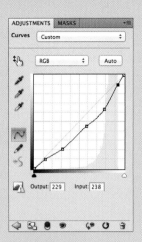

❸ Refining the Selection

Though the contrast between the suit and background is clearly defined, I still applied a slight feather to ensure that the Curves adjustment appeared natural and clean.

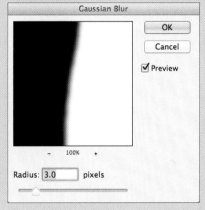

❹ Inverting the Selection

I wanted to increase the contrast between the background and suit. So, my next step was to darken the background. I made a copy of the previous layer and then inverted the layer mask (Command–I). With the mask active, I chose my Brush tool and, with black as my foreground color, I painted out the hands and head. I then applied a slight S-curve adjustment to increase the contrast and darken the background.

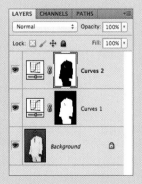

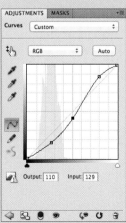

⑤ Adjusting the Skin

Again, I used the Magic Wand tool to select the hands and the head and created a new selection. From there, I created another Curves adjustment in which I focused on tweaking the dark tones and midtones. This provided a nice luminance to the skin that I was looking for. I then combined the Adjustment layers in a new layer by hitting Command + Option + Shift + E.

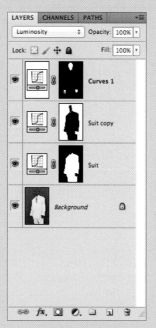

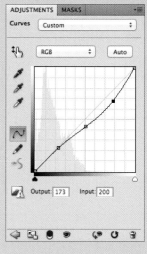

⑥ Adding a Lighting Effect

I knew that I wanted the lighting to appear much more dramatic than it was when I made the image, so I decided to add a lighting effect. To begin the process, I created a new layer and filled it with black.

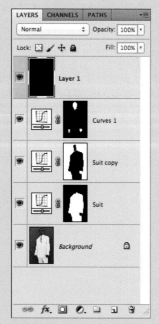

❼ Add Light Effect

I then went to Menu > Filter > Lighting Effects. I chose for my style, the Soft Omni effect, positioned it slightly behind his head. I Increased the intensity to 95% and made slight changes to the other settings until I got what I was looking for.

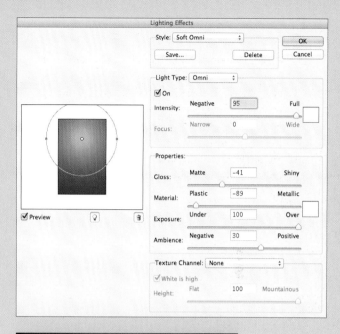

❽ Masking the Lighting Effect

I then moved the previous layer over the lighting-effect layer that I'd just created. I then copied the mask from my second Curves adjustment and used it for my lighting-effect layer. In this way, only the back-ground would be impacted by the effect.

9 Filter Effect

I wanted to add a glowing painterly effect to my subject's skin and background, so I choose Filter > Brush Strokes > Dark Strokes. I reduced the opacity to 41%, copied the previous layer mask, and added it to this new layer.

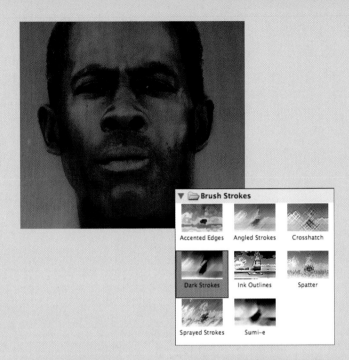

10 High Pass Filter

For the finishing touches, I combined the Adjustment layers in a new layer (Command + Option + Shift + E), and then I applied a High Pass Filter (Filter > Other > High Pass). I then changed the Blending Mode to Hard Light to increase detail contrast.

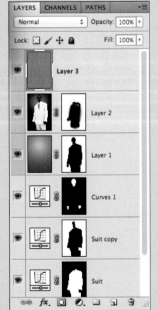

Conclusion

This final version of my image reflects the mood I was after and draws the viewer's eye to the aspects I find most compelling.

Riley Kern

"I want to evoke a little uneasiness in the viewer, along with intrigue."

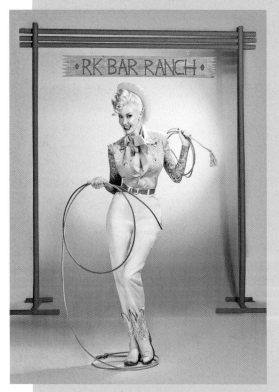

SABINAR, 2012

Imagery must first be born from my mind; a fantasy, delusion, or even just a whim can inspire me. I enjoy looking at eras long past and drawing inspiration from those while adding my own contemporary spin in my work. Movies, books, and stories are all a part of what keeps my mind fresh and my images flowing. Film Noir influences can be detected in much of the lighting I do for my fashion portraiture. However, my aim has shifted from making believable period pieces to making interesting imagery with an underlying retro vibe, all the while keeping an irony and sense of humor in much of the work.

I have become well known for my specialty with the classic pin-up cowgirl. Growing up in Bakersfield, "the honky-tonk of California," is the inspiration behind this campy work that brings me back to my roots, where I grew up watching *Hee Haw* and listening to Buck Owens. I always style my own shoots and have a large collection of western suits from the 40s and 50s that can often be found in my work.

I enjoy working in series as well. For example, I have a series called "Femme Fatale" that is just straight portraits, deadpan to the camera, highly stylized. The images are meant to portray businesswomen who have some more sinister ideas lurking just below the surface, portrayed in their mysterious stares at the audience. I want to evoke a little uneasiness in the viewer, along with intrigue. No matter what I am shooting, I always aim to make imagery that will provoke an emotion in the audience. I love to entertain, and the more over-the-top the story is, the happier I am.

Meganrenee, 2012

IVTYVWORK, 2012

LISACOWGRL, 2012

VICV3, 2008

VICMUG, 2008

IVYCWGRL, 2012

James Porto

"My goal is to make composite photographic images that...follow all the physical laws of a straight photograph, such as unity of perspective, light quality, and direction."

Untitled, 2008

At age 11, I fell in love with the black-and-white darkroom process at school. It didn't even matter which pictures I printed, as long as I had a negative to print. I developed a hunger to print more interesting negatives and turned my attention to that most essential aspect of photography, taking pictures.

I set out to master the techniques that would free me to create images I saw in my dreams but didn't exist in reality. I developed a system of seamlessly combining images on color film through a laborious darkroom process. Now the imagery in my mind could be convincingly rendered to film, but each image would take at least a month to complete due to the complex process.

Adobe Photoshop made it possible to perfectly transmute the darkroom process into a digital process. Finally, my dreams could be made real! For the last 20 years I've employed my style of photorealistic photo compositing for magazines, advertisements, books, and fine art images.

My goal is to make composite photographic images that have graphic visual impact, that possess a narrative to engage the viewer's intellect, are exciting and bold. Most importantly, I want my work to amaze and inspire people. The most direct way to accomplish this is to first amaze and inspire myself.

▶ Untitled, 2001

UNTITLED, 2010

UNTITLED, 2000

Richard Baxter

"The most interesting and successful artists...make art about what obsesses them, and in this very process they make the most interesting art for the world."

Artists do not expand the world; they present a smaller and more narrow view of it, which focuses our attention. What we see every day of our lives, surrounded by millions of other things, becomes more interesting when a small fragment is presented within a setting that isolates it, like a gallery, screen, frame, or even an ideology or style. Although we may have previously dimly noticed what the artist has presented, we have not isolated it enough to really view it closely with focused attention. The art gives us a space and reason to focus, concentrate, think, or just be aware.

Although having been obsessed with the visual since childhood, to this day I find it impossible to neatly categorize what I do in a statement. I make images. There is no goal, no philosophy, no ideas on what art should or shouldn't be. I would not like to be bound by ideals or habit, even though I realize certain waves of natural karma perpetuate through their own momentum.

Those waves play themselves out gradually until one is bored, until the energy is transformed into something else. All art is nothing but communication, and communication can happen in any medium in myriad ways. What interests me the most is this: Who, or what, is doing the communicating, and why?

At the heart of all my art, and probably all art, is the question: Who am I? If this question is successfully raised in any medium, the inquiry has been worthwhile. The most interesting and successful artists are the most selfish: They make art about what obsesses them, and in this very process they make the most interesting art for the world. It's a win-win.

THE DUMB GIANT AND THE TINY DANCER, 2007

DIVE, 2008

SHIP, 2009

SLEEPER, 2008

ECONOMY CLASS, 2009

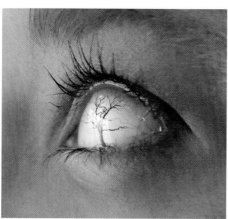

I SIGHT, 2009

Creating a Stormy Composite

The original idea for this image was a house in the rain and at a different angle. I did try using rain effects at first; however, I was unable to get the results I wanted and so gave up the idea completely, settling for a dark and wet landscape instead. Next, I needed a house, and so pored over my millions of personal stock images to find what I wanted. I didn't find the angle I wanted, but the house I did find was better than my original idea, as it was falling apart, thus giving a more interesting feel to the image that I hadn't quite imagined at first.

1 **Preparing the Shot**

The old house was photographed in a field, which I could not access from the road, and so the only image I had of it contained foliage in front of the house. This had to be removed in Photoshop using the Clone tool, and, essentially, I had to make up parts of the house using the Clone and Brush tools.

2 **Making the Selection**

I then carefully selected the house using the polygonal Lasso tool. Next, I feathered the selection (Select > Modify > Feather) with a pixel factor of 1 to slightly soften the edge of the mask. I removed the background, and then I created a new layer containing only the house.

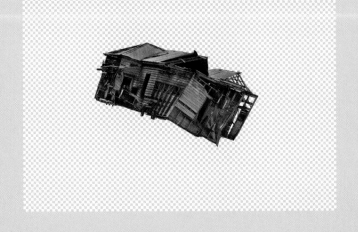

❸ Choosing the Background

I added a background image of a landscape behind the house.

❹ Matching Images

As it was, the house was too bright and did not match the darkness of the background, and because I wanted the feel of a dark and rainy day, I lowered the levels of the house until the lighting matched the background.

5 **Adding Elements**

For the clouds I used three separate photographs of clouds to make up the rich complexity of sky I was looking for. The last layer of cloud was used only on the right-hand side to lighten the sky a little. The cloud layer of Figure 6 was set to a filter level of Hard Light, which gave it the right effect. However, these filters change very much depending on what order the layers are in, so just play around with different settings for the layers until you find something that looks good.

6 Making Clouds

The lower patches of cloud or fog on the horizon were done by hand using the Airbrush tool. I use a graphics tablet, which gives me all the pressure control of using a real brush. This kind of effect would be very hard to do using a mouse, but not impossible.

Brushed by hand

7 Adding Details

The underside was put together using various elements. Some parts were objects I had already created in Photoshop and used in other projects, like the posts and the roots. Others were simply 2D cutouts of dark shapes designed to fill a space. The various parts are slightly separated before being put together under the house, which has been turned off in this picture.

⑧ Adding the Bird and the Telephone Pole

The birds were separate photographs added one by one. Each bird was photographed against a bright sky and was essentially a silhouette, so by setting the filter level of each bird layer to Multiply, the lightest areas behind the birds (the sky) were automatically made invisible, leaving only the dark areas of the birds themselves. The telephone pole was added in the same way as the house itself, having been previously photographed and cut out using the selection tool. It also had to have the levels adjusted in order for its lighting to look correct.

⑨ Adding Textures

I added a very slight texture to the entire scene. This texture had been created previously using many different layers to create a soft, warm, and complex texture. But you could use any texture you might have photographed as it is. I wanted an even texture in this case, so I created my own and have a large collection for use in images such as this.

Conclusion

The use of the texture is subtle, but it adds a warm and rich feel to the image. I added two layers of the same texture here, with one layer rotated 180 degrees for an even greater richness and subtlety. Both layers were set to 18% opacity; one layer was set to Overlay and the second to Multiply. You play around with these filters until you find the desired effect; there are so many combinations of levels and effects that it would be impossible to set a rule for them. I tend to favour Multiply myself, but that's only a personal choice.

Nick Vedros

"With a simple phrase, I put four sides around an idea. I launched a career."

Key Farm, 2008

I vividly remember at age 13 seeing my Uncle Mike's black-and-white photographs on the family kitchen table. It was as if a door opened for me. I announced that night to my family that I wanted to be a professional photographer when I grew up. This inspiration stayed with me through my graduation from the University of Missouri with a degree in Photojournalism. Once I moved into the realm of commercial photography I found my true passion. I live for assignments, but in between those projects I shoot my own concepts.

With a simple phrase, I put four sides around an idea. I launched a career. Anyone can look through a viewfinder, but there is nothing simple about bringing a concept to life. It takes inspired imagination fueled by ingenuity and a state-of-the-art production facility, with a team of handpicked professionals to execute these ideas to perfection.

▶ Walter with Crucifix Tattoo, 2003

CONEY ISLAND BOARDWALK, 2011

DC-3 AIRPLANE, 2009

CUTTING CATTLE AT FALLEN RANCH, 2009

MONTANA HOMESTEAD, 2012

DEJOE'S BACK STUDY, 2004

Brooke Shaden

"Why not explore the depths of the mind and soul and reach for something deeper than the reality that plagues us and traps us daily?"

AWAY FOR AGES, 2010

My goal in photography is to make beautiful that which others find disturbing, to take a simple concept (be it birth, death, or something in between—life) and mold it into something complex and magnetic.

My photographs are meant to be read and analyzed. Symbolism is abundant in them, for what makes an intricate story if not visuals that mean one thing but stand for another? Our world is not so different from the disturbing worlds I create within my frames. I argue that my surrealistic images are even more representational of life because they contain feelings and emotions that resonate with the viewers. Sometimes life does not have to be photographed according to reality. Instead, why not explore the depths of the mind and soul and reach for something deeper than the reality that plagues us and traps us daily?

My edited photographs are a far cry from the original image that comes out of the camera. I add texture to them to give a feeling of grime and age, thus giving the photographs a timeless feeling. I often play with the tones so that the subject is highlighted and the scenery falls away into slight desaturation and abandonment. The real crux of my photography is portraiture; it is capturing the emotion of a single instance in a life.

I want my imagery to move beyond the realm of photography and instead mimic paintings and alternate styles of art. I am not in love with any particular medium of art as much as I am in love with visually representing the stories in my mind. My photographs reflect a feeling that touches on the juxtaposition of the real yet surreal, a fantasy and a dream, yet riddled with reality.

A STORM TO MOVE MOUNTAINS, 2011

REACHING FOR CLOUDS, 2012

TO BEG FOR FIRE, 2012

The Buoyancy in Drowning, 2011

Tony Sweet

"There is a direct correlation between seeing and playing improvised music. In both I am editing in the midst of spontaneity, and I'm continually learning from experience."

FLOWER TEXTURE, 2010

I discovered photography after 20 years as a professional jazz musician. As I like to say, I started late, and I learned fast. Photography for me has been a lot like jazz: composing on the spot in the midst of fluid and constantly changing conditions, but the only difference are the tools that I'm using. It's all about finding and getting caught in the moment.

When I discovered photography and made those first slides, I knew that I could be good at this. Miles Davis said, "When you see something that you can do, you know it immediately." That's what photography was and has been for me. For me, there is a direct correlation between seeing and playing improvised music. In both I am editing in the midst of spontaneity, and I'm continually learning from experience. I've learned that it's not always good to include everything just because it's there. There's beauty to be found when one is more selective, leaving and working with more space. This happens in music, but it also sounds like pictures to me.

Nothing creative is conscious. The best moments of photography are when I've stepped into the moment and completely freed my mind. The moment I start thinking about it too much, the moment is gone. One cannot think as fast as one reacts.

Fisgard Lighthouse, 2012

ZIMMERMAN'S FARM, 2008

▶ PEGGY'S COVE LIGHT, 2004

CLINGMAN'S OVERLOOK, 2012

ICELAND CHURCH PATHWAY, 2010

Enhancing the Details

As part of a long-term project photographing downtown Los Angeles, I have produced several images that detail some of the architecture, particularly the classic movie palaces that line Broadway. The weathered surfaces in this shot piqued my interest, but the flat lighting diminished their impact. So, I knew that I would need to work on this image in Photoshop to bring out the fine details that drew my attention to the scene.

1 **Working the RAW file**

After opening the image in the Adobe Raw Converter (ARC), I corrected the off-kilter framing of the original shot as well as slightly improved the overall contrast, but especially with the midtones, with a touch of Clarity.

② Global Contrast

The overcast lighting resulted in a flat look to all the elements in the photograph. Though I intended to do more localized contrast control, I started off with a slight Curves adjustment to increase the overall contrast.

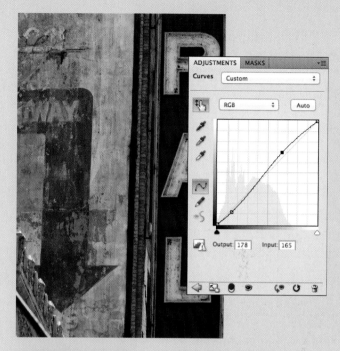

③ Luminosity Blending Mode

I changed the blending mode to Luminosity so that the contrast would not produce any color shift.

④ Working with Color Range

I wanted to brighten and increase the contrast of the letters of the marquee. To do this, I created another Curves layer. To localize the changes only to the letter, I went to Menu > Select > Color Range and used the eyedropper tool to select the white lettering. I then refined the selection using the Fuzziness and Range sliders.

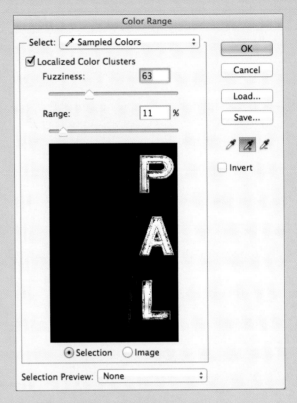

⑤ Increase Contrast in Lettering

Now with a mask created for the lettering, I changed the Curves adjustment to increase the contrast, which helped brighten the lettering and increase the contrast within the letters themselves. I then changed the blending mode to Luminosity.

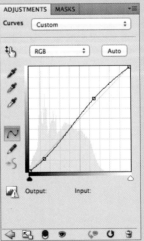

6 Hue/Saturation Adjustment Layer

Because I wanted to eliminate the yellow color cast within the lettering, I created a Hue/Saturation Adjustment layer. I then copied the layer mask from the previous layer and applied it to the new Adjustment layer. I then reduced the color saturation and slightly increased the lightness.

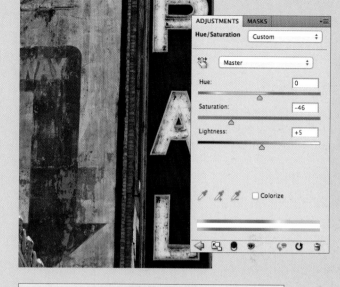

7 Color Range Control

I wanted to improve the look of the arrow on the surface of the wall. After creating a Curves adjustment, I used the Color Range control (Menu > Select > Color Range). I then selected and refined the selection using the Fuzziness and Range sliders.

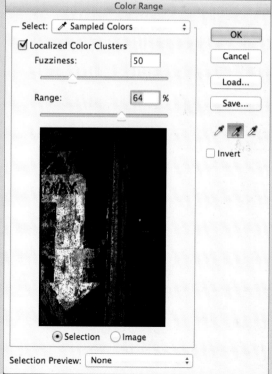

8 **Improving the Arrow and Applying High Pass**

I made a Curves adjustment and changed the blending mode to Hard Light. Then I merged the Adjustment Layers in a new layer (Command + Option + Shift + E). To reveal the abundant texture within the shot, I went to Menu > Filter > Other > High Pass and adjusted the radius to emphasize the details I wanted.

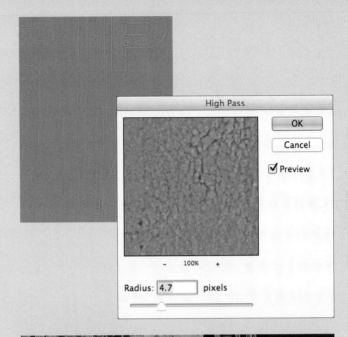

9 **Refining the High Pass Filter**

To fine-tune the effect, I changed the blending mode to Hard Light and reduced the opacity to 86%.

⑩ Refining Contrast

I still wanted to pursue the contrast further, so I created a Color Mixer Adjustment layer. With the monochrome option selected, I adjusted the red, green, and blue sliders until I got a good-looking, high-contrast black-and-white version of the image.

⑪ Using the Blending Mode

I then converted the Blending Mode to Luminosity, which dramatically improved the contrast while maintaining the colors. As you can see, I've used luminosity repeatedly, especially when I want to control contrast with these layers.

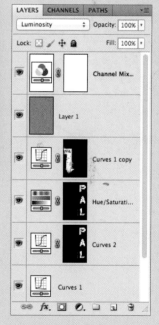

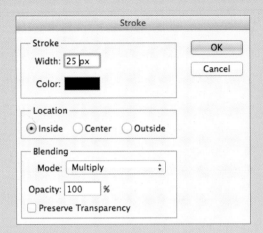

⑫ Finishing the Image with a Border

For the finishing touch, I wanted to create a black border around the image. I combined the previous layers into a new layer (Command + Option + Shift + E). I then went to Menu > Edit > Stroke and created a stroke of 25 pixels and checked off the Inside menu option.

Conclusion

The final result emphasizes the colors and textures that drew my attention to the scene. It becomes my interpretation of the weathered signage.

Jim Kazanjian

"I'm interested in occupying a space where the mundane intersects the strange, and the familiar becomes alien."

<small>UNTITLED CHATEAU, 2011</small>

My images are digitally manipulated composites built from photographs I find online. The technique I use could almost be considered *hyper-collage.* I cobble together pieces from photos I find interesting and feed them into Photoshop. Through a palimpsest-like layering process of adding and subtracting, I gradually blend the various parts together. I am basically manipulating and assembling a disparate array of multiple photographic elements to produce a single homogenized image.

My method of construction has an improvisational and random quality to it, since it is largely driven by the source material I have available. Each new piece I bring to the composition informs the image's potential direction. It is an iterative and organic process where the end result is many times removed from its origin. I think of the work as a type of mutation that can haphazardly spawn in numerous and unpredictable directions.

I've chosen photography as a medium because of the cultural misunderstanding that it has a sort of built-in objectivity. This allows me to set up a visual tension within the work, to make it resonate and lure the viewer further inside. My current series is inspired by the classic horror literature of H.P. Lovecraft, Algernon Blackwood, and similar authors. I am intrigued with the narrative archetypes these writers utilize to transform the commonplace into something sinister and foreboding. In my work, I prefer to use these devices as a means to generate entry points for the viewer. I'm interested in occupying a space where the mundane intersects the strange, and the familiar becomes alien.

Untitled Implosion, 2008

UNTITLED LOW TIDE, 2009

UNTITLED TOMB, 2012

UNTITLED STRUCTURE, 2007

UNTITLED HOUSE, 2006

Gediminas Pranckevičius

> "We're all just a little bit crazy inside, and I take all my ideas from that little crazy part of me."

My name is the same as that of the famous knight of Lithuania who built our capital city. So, I'm trying to be a knight of the computer graphics world.

We're all just a little bit crazy inside, and I take all my ideas from that little crazy part of me. Painting and creating is a never-ending way of life for me. I often compare it to playing a video game with an infinite number of levels and possibilities. But instead of vying for the highest score, I gain satisfaction by my use of color, shapes, and composition. My imagination inspires me to discover new and exciting ways of expressing the images that begin like a spark in my mind.

REMBRANDT, 2011

▶ TIME, 2012

UNTITLED BACKGROUND, 2011

AUTUMN, 2012

THE LITTLE MATCH GIRL, 2011

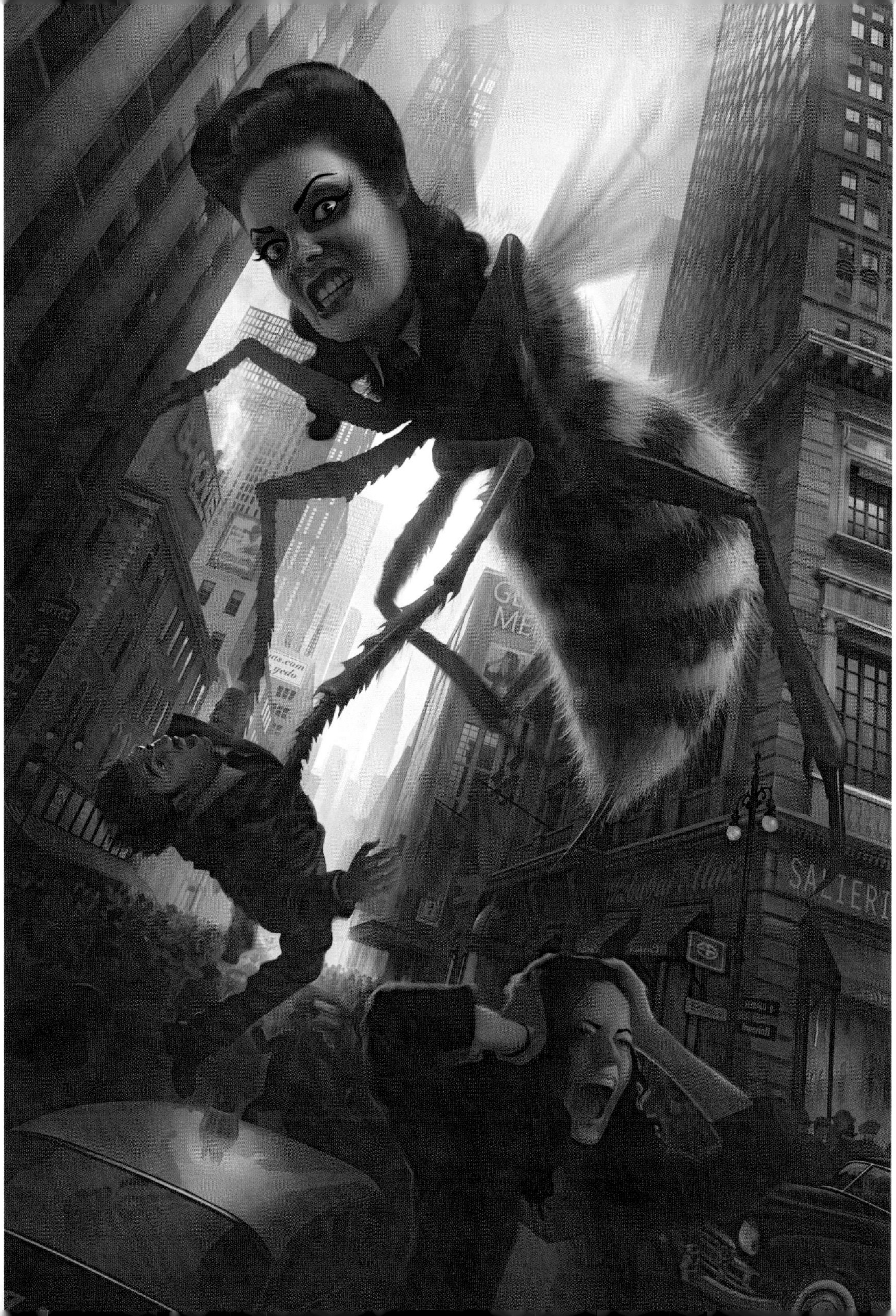

Wasp Women,
2010

Monster by Moonlight

For better or worse, the werewolf is a popular character in horror. Though frequently visualized as something very evil, I thought I'd do a different take on this monster and create something that was a little less horrifying.

1 **Sketching the Idea**

Using Photoshop, I quickly created a sketch. Composition and proportion were the least important at this point. Sometimes it helps a lot to completely relax at the initial stage. I had an urgent need to see a lovely wolf in an awkward situation.

2 **Brushing in Depth**

I then created a new layer and, using the Brush tool, I used shading to create a sense of depth as well evoke a sense of night. At this point, I merged those two layers and created a new one on top with the Multiply blending mode.

❸ Creating Volume

To create some volume, I used a standard round Brush tool, with its opacity set to 70%. I worked out the path of the light and darkened where it would naturally be darker. It's important to be patient at this stage and to just keep working. It's not a bad idea to duplicate this layer and just hide it, because later on it might save your life.

❹ Enhancing with Moonlight

A common saying goes, "Where shadows are there is light also." I'm working with light on another layer, and I painted those areas that should be illuminated by moonlight.

⑤ Enhancing with Moonlight

Now it's time for some additional details and textures. I created the moon and also included a victim in the hollow of a tree. After a brief play with details, I enhanced whole image using the Dodge and Burn tool to enhance highlights and shadows.

⑥ Adding Color

I then merged all the layers into a single layer and made a copy of it. I edited the top layer with the Curve tool (Ctrl + m) by decreasing the red and blue channels to achieve a bluish-green color. Having two layers allowed me to color trees by erasing some parts of the top layers.

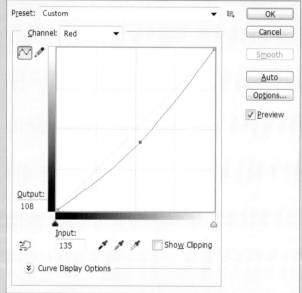

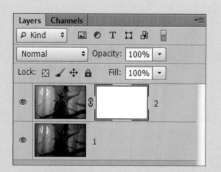

7 **Adding Leaves**

After so much hard work, it was time for dessert.
I created a new layer, and with a few small brushes
illuminated the forest with direct moonlight. A lack of
vegetation forced me to use the Leaves and Veggie
Brush Pack by Charfade.

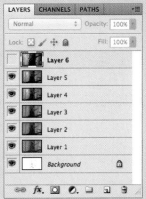

Conclusion

It's still a mystery to me why that poor fellow in the tree was wandering in the middle of the forest at night. Nevertheless, I believe everything will be just fine.

Sarah Wilmer with Mike Schultz

"After we had all of the paintings in the digital realm, we began marrying them to the photographs."

We decided to approach the subject matter through the lens of an apocalyptic world. By combining painting and photography we were able to transcend our own particular mediums. The result was a group of images depicting a post-apocalyptic world full of visions, apparitions, and mirages.

With each picture we wish to illustrate an idea. It could be an entity from a dream, an experience in everyday life, a vague feeling, a memory, a desire, fear, hope, inspiration from nature, the future, or even a childhood memory of playing Super Mario Brothers video game.

Objects can help to illustrate an idea either literally or symbolically. The unifying theme of all of the props in this series are a reimagined technology where all machinery on earth must begin again. For example, in the post-apocalyptic world you may need a helmet equipped with a large lamp to ward off hybrid animals.

We were working with actual photographs and oil paintings. After editing the photos to find the best body language and facial expressions, we began the process of combining the figures and the painted landscapes in Photoshop. After we had all of the paintings in the digital realm, we began marrying them to the photographs.

Some files ultimately would have around 20 to 30 image layers. Once we had the composition in a good place, we would begin working on color and density. The last step was minor painting touch-ups using various tools in Photoshop.

In general, we both tend to be very particular about our art, but together we have a natural kinship and work in a very open and cooperative way.

GOGGLE, 2008

BIKE, 2008

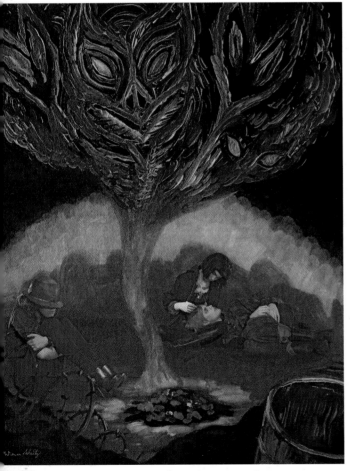

Boat, 2008

Fire, 2008

▶ Untitled, 2009

Walter Plotnick

> "I am able to visually explore an abstract environment with objects and light, creating movement, form, and tension."

My current work is a hybrid of wet photography and digital process. I make photographs and photograms by constructing temporary still lifes using vintage found objects and images on top of photographic paper in the darkroom. By manipulating a variety of light sources, and then digitally combining, repeating, or adding images, I am able to visually explore an abstract environment with objects and light, creating movement, form, and tension.

Photography is a form of communication with the power to move, inspire, and motivate people. Two areas of inquiry have fascinated me with their graphic possibilities: the *World of Tomorrow*-themed 1939 New York World's Fair, and vintage images depicting feats of daring by 1930s circus performers. On the surface, these are two disparate themes, but for me the commonality is humanity striving to reach its potential. The 1939 New York World's Fair presented this on a grand stage, showing what was possible in technology with the right vision and will, engaging science, commerce, and government in an inspiring display of imagination. The circus performers, with little or no technology, took us to the outer limits of skill and performance using only the human body. Together, they offer us a thrilling picture of what we can do when we have the faith to leap forward to the next level.

Faith, inspiration, and achievement are the hallmarks of human accomplishment. I feel that through creating images that celebrate these themes, my images will resonate with viewers, and hopefully awaken in them an appreciation for their potential and expand a sense of what is possible in their own lives.

PLOTNICK CIRCUS SERIES 1, 2007

PLOTNICK NUDE STUDY, 2008

PLOTNICK OPTICAL BRIDGE, 2008

PLOTNICK WORLDS FAIR 2, 2012

PLOTNICK CIRCUS SERIES 2, 2007

PLOTNICK SCREEN GEM, 2007

PLOTNICK CIRCUS SERIES 6, 2009

Erik Almas

> "The idea of becoming a photographer is now my reality, and I'm truly grateful."

Photography fell in my lap, almost as if it rained on me. I didn't have a great interest in pictures or art. And a relative didn't give me a camera when I was 12. Rather, random forces seemed to strike me in different places. When I finally reached a crossroad and asked myself: "What do I do now?," I became consumed by the idea of becoming a photographer. Since then, small encounters have led me halfway across the world and then around it a few times.

I grew up in Trondheim, Norway, a big city by Norwegian standards but barely a blip on the map with its population of 150,000 people. I vividly remember the day I moved to the United States to study photography, flying in over the Bay Area at night. The lights went on forever. I was 22 and felt really small, intimidated by the number of lights and what they illuminated. I attended the Academy of Art University for four years and had some truly inspiring teachers who encouraged me to change my goal from shooting sporting events for my hometown newspaper to wanting to create great images. I graduated in 1999 with Best Portfolio in the Spring Show. As an assistant for almost three years, I became inspired and encouraged. I then nurtured my own image-making talents and developed work habits that have helped me succeed on my own. I'm glad I can say I've succeeded. The idea of becoming a photographer is now my reality, and I'm truly grateful. I ended up staying in San Francisco, where I've lived for 13 years. I shoot pictures, and I'm too happy doing it, trying to make today's photos better than yesterday's.

Personal Camel, 2011

AMTRAK CUP, 2008

NOMAD, 2008

ITALY MONASTERY, 2005

Dean West

> "I am not so much a photographer as somebody who uses photography to bring his visions to life."

My artist statement continually evolves, along with my work. I would have to say that I am not so much a photographer as somebody who uses photography to bring his visions to life.

POOL, 2009

Production, 2011

TREE, 2012

CREATIVE CONCEPTING, 2011

UMBRELLA, 2011

QUEEN OF THEBES, 2011

Star Foreman

> " I am very much a product of Los Angeles, a city that exists in a time vacuum that encompasses the future, past, and present in one place. "

The reality my images portray is slightly skewed from average. Visually my work owes a great deal to the Technicolor cinema of the 30s–60s, with the greatest debt being to the tricolor process employed by artists such as Cecil Beaton and Madame Yevonde. Predicated by the common visual language that years of film viewing has instilled in us, the viewers, my work can feel both familiar and utterly new.

When creating an homage—such as Technicolor Mucha—I am obsessed with details, trying to create a work that is both new and a perfect recreation of the original. When creating purely from my imagination, I am a visual improvisator, placing items, people, and lights in and out, sometimes leaving people where they are but moving myself, circling them, working toward an image that can satisfy what should be.

I grew up in the world of theater (my grandfather was a theater critic and my uncle an actor). Every summer day I would alternate swimming in my grandparents' pool and watching American movie classics. Somehow this fusion of the bright Southern California light, glamour of classic movies, and hundreds of nights watching stage shows at every level of competency created the reality I love to create. I now style much of my own work from my enormous vintage Hollywood costume closet, with pieces gleaned from Paramount and Warner Bros. studios.

I am very much a product of Los Angeles, a city that exists in a time vacuum that encompasses the future, past, and present in one place. So many of my images, even though they are bright and colorful, have a desperate undercurrent of loneliness, with subjects who interact but never connect. My images are steeped in color, whimsy, isolation, intimacy, innovation, cinema, and the city that is my home, Los Angeles.

Mad Hatter and White Rabbit, 2012

▶ Maleficent and Aurora, 2012

TECHNICOLOR MUCHA, 2010

ALISON BRIE AS ROSIE THE RIVETER, 2011

RE: HAROLD LLOYD, 2011

BITE THE APPLE, 2012

BLUE FAIRY, 2012

Miss Aniela

"I want to stir people to question and to *think*, intelligibly, about the problems, the beauty, and the conflict between them in the world around us."

MIGRATION SEASON, 2012

I pour my mind into everything I create. I aim to push the envelope with compelling imagery and the highest production value, whether I'm shooting with a huge budget or with my own body and a remote trigger. Photography is always my "living," whether I am working on personal or commercial work, because creating keeps me feeling alive.

My series *Ecology* is about our world and the place of humanity within it, at once a beautiful and polluting form. The images play with growth and disruption of growth, with utopia and its opposite, dystopia. In this series, I want to stir people to question and to *think*, intelligibly, about the problems, the beauty, and the conflict between them in the world around us. The images are an evolution of my playful self-portraiture from 2006–2009; it is a way to express a troubled outlook on the world, through quietly sinister and even unnerving distortions.

In my *Surreal Fashion* series, fashion portraits become immersed into fine-art surrealism. I make bizarre interactions between models and other elements, such as paintings, drawings, and objects found in the location in which the model was shot. The surroundings of the model echo, distort, and appear in unexpected ways in each situation. This is my attempt as a fine-art photographer at making fashion-shoot situations more artistic, imaginative, and thought-provoking, and to take the easily mimicked "in-camera" fashion shot several innovative stages further.

DELIVERANCE, 2011

THE ESCAPE, 2008

REVERIE, 2008

STORM DOOR, 2011

152 ANIELA

THEIR EVENING BANTER, 2008

Body Repairs

This image, on first glance, is striking for its thriller-like scenario and the narrative questions it invokes as to how the subject has achieved a particular pose in an ominous setting. The image's surrealism lies in its subtle use of manipulation: The woman's position is not necessarily impossible—but definitely uncomfortable. A strategic placing of props in the original image, and post-production in Photoshop to remove the photographer's assistant, resulted in an image that effectively conveys a sense of the surreal without a blatant focus on the mechanics involved.

❶ Making the Initial Shot with the Subject

This image was shot in a building-supplies warehouse in Los Angeles and features model Katie Johnson. The original shots show how the assistant held the chain in the air whilst the other end was wrapped around Katie, who was laying back on a stool. With great flexibility she was able to wrap herself back around the other side of the stool and allow her head to hang down to the floor.

❷ Making the Second Initial Shot Without the Subject

I took another shot of the scene without Katie or the stool, which I used as a layer in the composite so I could remove the stool and the assistant.

❸ Overlaying the Empty Scene

I dragged in the image without the model and created a new layer. To get positioning correct, I reduced the opacity so that I could view the position of both images and align them properly.

❹ Removing the Unnecessary

The objective was easy to achieve in terms of having Katie appear to be hanging without an aid. I set the brush on black (soft-edged, but zoomed in close) to reveal the body of Katie whilst leaving the stool invisible.

5 **Cropping**

Although I usually leave cropping to the last stage, I cropped this image at an early stage to leave out distracting boxes that were on the left of the original image. This instantly made the model more central, and, given that I was unsure when first editing this image, it went in favor of the image's inaugural sense of progress.

6 **Working the Background**

The hardest part was making the image look effective and interesting contextually and aesthetically. Having shot this image in dark surroundings, but wanting to retain the exposure of the model, I reopened the background image in Camera Raw and worked on a separate exposure file for the background. I excessively lightened, denoised, and added vibrancy, and then I layered it into the shot. This gave a painterly quality to the background without affecting the foreground, in the manner of a manual HDR.

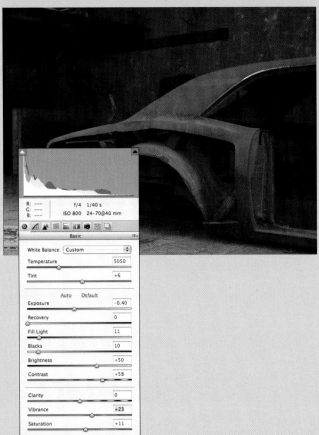

7 Improving Details

I also took an extra piece of hair from another shot of Katie on the ground to make it seem as though her curls surrounded her all the way round her head, filling the gap in the middle. I added this as another layer and carefully positioned and blended it to look natural.

8 Adding the Shadow

I brought the missing shadow back into the image by making a feathered selection and darkening it using a Levels adjustment. Feathering the mask is important in order to create a soft-looking shadow that appears to have occurred naturally.

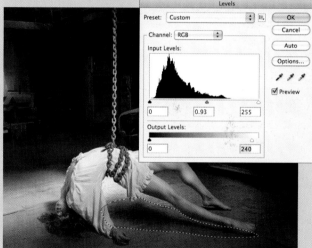

⑨ Improving Contrast

I boosted the impact of the overall image by adjusting colors in Curves. By creating a slight S-Curve, I was able to increase the overall contrast of the shot. Even a small change can be enough to considerably improve the contrast of a photograph.

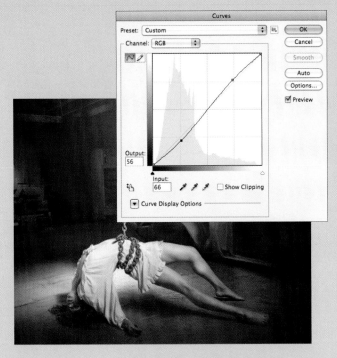

⑩ Luminosity Blending Mode

To avoid the adjustment in contrast affecting color, I switch the blending mode from Normal to Luminosity, which will apply the Curves adjustment only to the luminance channel.

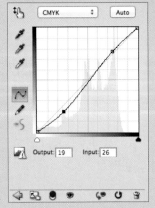

⑪ Adding a Vignette

To emphasize the subject at the center of the frame, I added a vignette using Lens Distortion. The darkening of the edges of the frame helps guide the viewer's eye. However, I made the effort to make sure that the vignette appears as subtle and natural as possible.

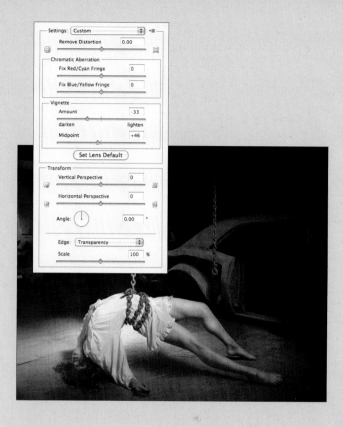

⑫ Finishing Touches

I was very happy with the overall look, but I wanted to emphasize her mouth more. So I enhanced the red of the model's lips by making a selection around them and increasing the Reds in Hue and Saturation.

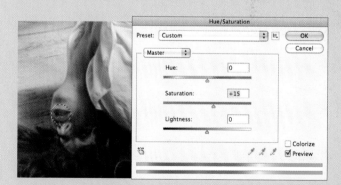

Conclusion

And here's the resulting image. A strategic placing of props in the original image and post-production in Photoshop resulted in an image that effectively conveys a sense of the surreal without a blatant focus on the mechanics involved.

Valp Maciej Hajnrich

"Valp uses a combination of photography manipulation and hand-drawn effects to make his ideas a reality."

Characterized by bright colors and a vibrant energy, the creations of this self-styled *graphic illusionist* are unlike anything his contemporaries are doing and have been featured on websites, album covers, TV ads, and even London buses.

Valp Maciej Hajnrich has a passion for his chosen vocation, and what began as a hobby 15 years ago has grown into a fulfilling career. The self-taught artist takes his inspiration from the visuals in the world around him, from static to motion, ancient to contemporary, and he uses a combination of photography manipulation and hand-drawn effects to make his ideas a reality. He extensively researches every piece he is commissioned for to ensure the right effects are achieved and the correct message conveyed.

ESPN Skylar, 2011

▶ Tomorrow Never Happened, 2011

Live Your Passion, 2011

Trust the Future, 2008

PRISCILLA, 2008

WINTER ESPIONAGE, 2007

Sean Teegarden

"I use digital imaging to explore the impossible, going against the laws of physics that analog photography is heavily limited by."

RECORD PLAYER, 2010

Master painters of old would paint in the flaws on their subjects as a finishing touch, a method of making paintings real. My personal work is never intended to be a literal interpretation of reality. I was molded to believe there is an idealistic life that we should pursue at any cost. Some people believe chasing this life will ultimately result in some sort of utopian existence, but what we really end up with is damage under the surface from struggling to maintain appearances.

I have always been fascinated by the post-war modern era that exemplified these beliefs. There was a time when anything was possible and new ideas were exploding into existence. The world was good and America was great, or so it would seem. Midcentury Americana is a representation of dreams and improbable realities. Now, through an idealistic lens, many view the world the way it used to be, but probably never was. Just like our memories, art tells a story of an impression, not of a fact.

Storytelling comes in many forms, and photography is an ideal medium for narrative. I believe excellent production values can give focus to the message. I use digital imaging to explore the impossible, going against the laws of physics that analog photography is heavily limited by. Photoshop gives my process several tools not available in traditional mediums, specifically blend modes for treatment and paths combined with channels for selection methods. These tools, when used in balance, produce exceptional photo illustration and allow my idealistic vision to become a reality.

▶ HOPALONG, 2010

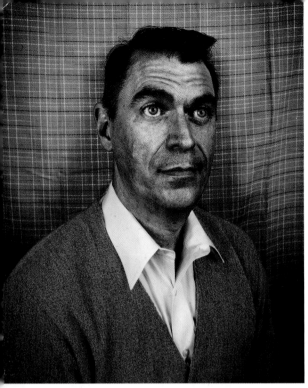

Detecto, 2010

Art, 2010

My Dad

Bethany, 2010

▶ David Lynch, 2010

Blend Modes and Layer Masks, an Unbeatable Combination

Blending modes are of equal importance to masking and, when paired together, make for an endless combination of interesting and exciting possibilities. Basically, blend modes allow layers to interact with each other in unique ways (different from opacity or fill), based on the variables of the layer content, i.e., color, contrast, and brightness.

1 **Introducing the Two Key Blend Modes**

For this image, we will use two blend modes that are especially useful for compositing, Multiply and Screen. These two modes allow certain layer content to take on the appearance of transparency without the need for complex masking. Multiply and Screen are opposites of each other, and, as such, live in separate categories: darkening and lightening.

❷ The Portrait

For the portrait, we have a spaceman on a silver background, and even though his treatment is almost complete, the background is in need of some aging and texture.

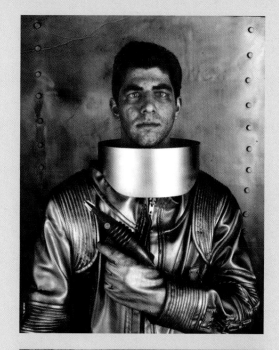

❸ Photographing Textures

I decided to blend a shot of some rust onto the background. I often shoot images that involve texture and color with the specific intent of possibly blending them later with other images.

4 Multiply Blending Mode

The first inclination is to reduce opacity or to mask out the bright parts of the image. Though both of these options can be mixed in, the most efficient starting point is to use the blend mode Multiply. When a layer is placed in Multiply, its dark pixels are applied to the layers below and its light pixels disappear. This mode is great for laying on dark textures (like our rust) or shadows on surfaces as if they were always in the image.

5 Masking the Layer

When the rust layer is used in combination with a layer mask, the texture can be constrained to specific areas of the image, making the effect local, not global.

6 Adding the Helmet

Now, what spaceman would be complete without a bubble helmet? An intricate mask could be attempted to select just the highlight area of the bubble; however, the blend mode Screen will get the layer to blend very well into the composite. When a layer is placed in Screen, its light pixels are applied to the layers below and its dark pixels disappear. This mode is great for compositing clear objects like our helmet or glassware. It's also great for weather effects like rain or snow.

7 Increasing Visibility

We can also use a Levels adjustment on the helmet to increase visibility in certain areas. Though this is often used for brightening an image or increasing contrast, it becomes an invaluable tool for refining the look of the helmet.

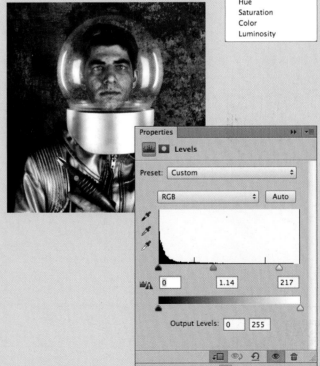

8 **Removing Highlights**
We then create a layer mask to remove the highlights from crucial features on the model.

Conclusion

Although it might be less work to just photograph the helmet on the spaceman instead of putting the images together in Photoshop, I preferred photographing them separately. It enabled me to change the quality of lighting for the portrait in a different way from the helmet, ensuring that the highlights on the dome didn't obscure the subject's face. Sometimes the physics of light don't allow for optimal placement and direction on all elements in an image, and programs like Photoshop allow the impossible to become successful pieces of art and design.

Maki Kawakita

"The explosive use of color, graphics, and storytelling elements produce...a stage on which she explores issues of identity and modern pop culture."

Maki Kawakita's work is inspired and informed by many influences, including traditional and modern Western and Japanese cultures. In her modern take on Shibuya Pop culture, one can not only see hints of today's Manga, but also the medieval Japanese tradition of Emaki, a picture roll that combines both text and images to produce a sequential visual narrative.

She combines elements of illustration and photography for dramatic effect and vibrant layouts that reflect the hyperreality of today's youth culture. The influences of Western culture can be found within her imagery, reflecting a culture's pursuit of a unique and distinct identity.

The explosive use of color, graphics, and storytelling elements produce visually compelling images and a stage on which she explores issues of identity and modern pop culture. Her images are powerful hybrids that result from the conflicting merger of East and West.

MAKIRAMA 4, 2005

▶ MAKIRAMA 2, 2005

Shibuya Pop 3, 2012

Makirama 8, 2005

Shibuya Pop 4, 2012

Makirama 5, 2005

Ibarionex Perello

> "My awareness of light and dark, contrast and tonality inform…how I use applications like Photoshop to guide the viewer's eye… to emphasize what I believe is important."

One of the greatest pleasures that I derive from photography is the process of finding the extraordinary in the ordinary. Whether I discover it in an ordinary urban street corner or in the face of a complete stranger, the camera provides me the opportunity to capture and share that sense of discovery, which makes the act of photography such a fascinating process for me.

In many ways, my photography is the practice of looking for those elements that reveal character, not only that possessed by a person, but by a city or a community. I then take those images and quietly and subtly control how the viewer experiences the final photograph. My awareness of light and dark, contrast and tonality inform not only how I shoot, but how I use applications like Photoshop to guide the viewer's eye in and around the frame to emphasize what I believe is important. When I am successful, I hope to provide the viewer with an aesthetically pleasing image, one that will make them aware of the fascinating things that surround us every waking moment but are ignored or so easily passed over. I hope that my images encourage people to stop and linger on the amazing things that are around us. And if nothing else, it helps me to be present in my own life, a huge challenge in a world filled with so much electronic noise. My images explore the real world and capture life as I see and experience it.

▶ BIBLE AND TEN, 2010

CROSSED LEGS IN BAR, 2011

THE REDHEAD, 2012

DRESS DUMMY ON BROADWAY, 2007

DAPPER, 2012

STREET ENCOUNTER, 2012

Guiding the Viewer Experience with Contrast

When I encountered this fellow on the streets of Los Angeles, I knew that I had to make a photograph of him. After getting his permission, I moved him near a wall, which provided an ideal background. Though the image that I captured in-camera was well-exposed and sharp, it was only my starting point. I knew that I would need to work on the image in Photoshop to build on its inherit strengths.

① Preparing the Raw File

I took the raw file and made some minor adjustments to the image in preparing it for my work in Photoshop. This included correcting for the slight underexposure as well as tweaking the white balance. I also included a modest amount of pre-sharpening and clarity to maintain the crispness to the image, which would be important to me.

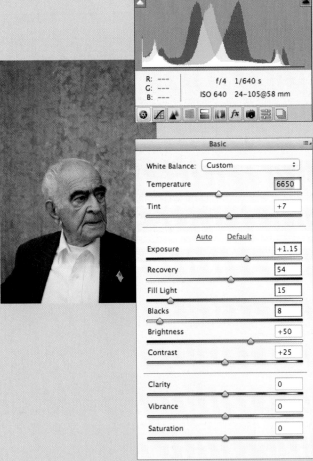

❷ Adjusting Global Contrast

Because I photographed my subject in an area of
open shade, I knew that the overall look of the image
would be a little flat. To remedy this, I created a
Levels Adjustment layer and moved in the black-and-
white sliders to establish my white and black points.
By depressing the Option/Alt key while moving the
sliders, I could see exactly where my brightest and
darkest areas of the frame were, ensuring that I
wouldn't lose too much detail in those extremes of
the tonal range.

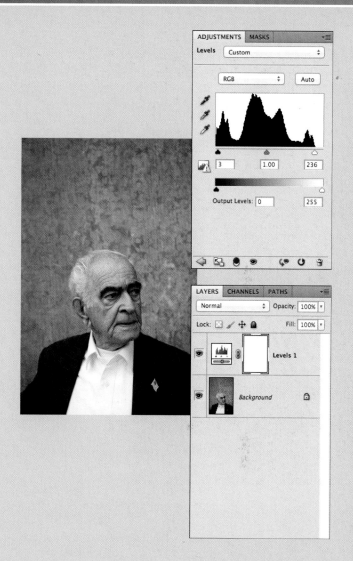

3 **Adjusting Local Contrast**

I knew that I wanted to darken the suit a bit, while increasing the brightness on his face. For that I created a Curves Adjustment Layer, which allowed me to selectively darken the lower quartertones, while slightly increasing my midtones. This increased the contrast between his white shirt and his suit, and helped to guide the viewer's eye to the center of the composition and his face.

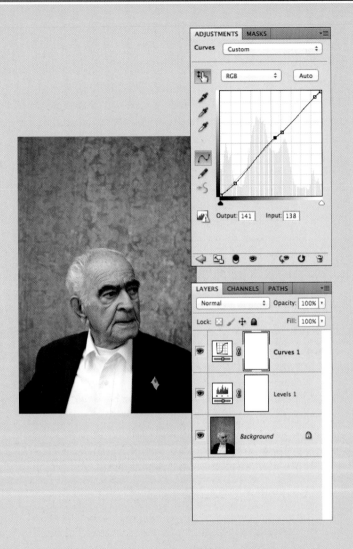

❹ Burning

Dodging and burning play a big role in my photo editing in both color and black-and-white. The ability to control brightness levels provides the means to guide the viewer through the frame. For this, I created a Burn layer by clicking on the New Layer icon at the bottom of the layers palette while holding down the Option/Alt key. I then went to the Mode option and selected Soft Light, and I clicked on the check box for Fill with Soft-light-neutral color (50% gray). I then chose the Brush tool, making black my foreground color, and, with an opacity of about 15%, selectively darkened the background for a more controlled vignette. I also darkened select areas of the suit as well as shadows on his shirt. I reduced the opacity to 5% and targeted the ears and far side of his face to emphasize the center.

❺ Dodging

Now it was time to selectively brighten areas of the image. Again, I clicked on the New Layer icon at the bottom of the layers palette, while holding down the Option/Alt key. I went to the Mode option and selected Soft Light. I then clicked on the check box for Fill with Soft-light-neutral color (50% gray). I selected the Brush tool and made white my foreground color. Again, I started off with an opacity of about 15%. This allowed me to brighten the white hair, the eyes, the lips, the center mass of his face and his American flag lapel pin. His hair was a critical consideration because his skin tone closely matched the color of the wall. So, the white hair provides a source of separation between him and the background.

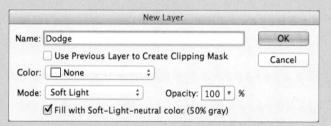

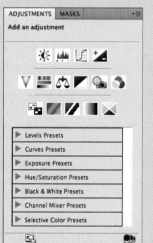

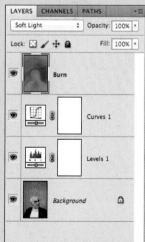

6 **The High-Contrast Approach**

The texture and details of his face were something that I was attracted to. I knew I wanted to emphasize this, but without overdoing it for other areas of the frame. So I created another Adjustment layer filled with gray, as I have with the previous two steps, but chose the Hard Light rather than Soft Light option. I then went to the menu bar to Filter > Other > High Pass. With the image magnified 50%, I adjusted the radius of the High Pass filter until I got a look in the detail in the eyebrows and hair that I was looking for, which was about 3.0. I didn't want to magnify noise too much, I just wanted to create a crisp look. I then created a layer mask filled with white and selected a brush with black as the foreground color. I then painted out the effect on those areas I didn't want influenced by the High Pass filter.

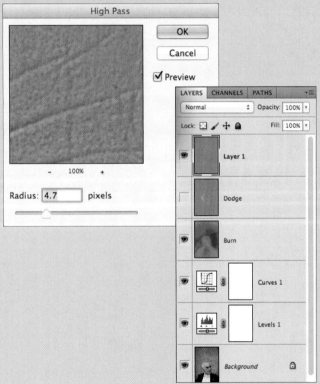

❼ The Black-and-White Filter Effect

I wanted to boost the contrast even more to provide some punch to the image, and one way that really works for me is to create a black-and-white Adjustment layer. I then tried the various black-and-white presets to find one that appealed to me, and selected the Blue filter. Though it looks like overkill right now, I'm not done.

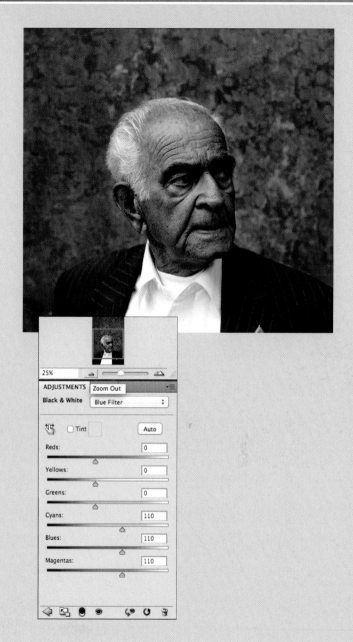

8 **The High-Contrast Approach**

I switched the blending mode from Normal to Luminosity, which means that the Adjustment layer is working on the luminance or black-and-white tones in the image. Next, I reduced the opacity of the layer until I found a sweet spot for the look of my image. In this case, I settled on 25%.

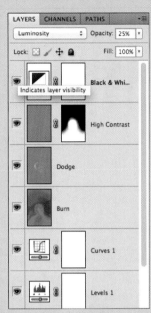

9 **Working the Eyes**

In the end, I thought I was losing some detail in the eyes. So, I made a selection around both eyes and created a new Curves adjustment layer. I applied a slight Gaussian blur to the mask. I then created a slight Curves adjustment that brightened the whites of the eyes, but that maintained the darkness of the pupils.

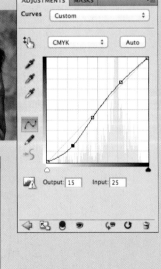

Conclusion

The final result captures what I had in mind when I created the photograph. It really emphasizes the man's great features and the obvious pride and dignity in which he carried himself.

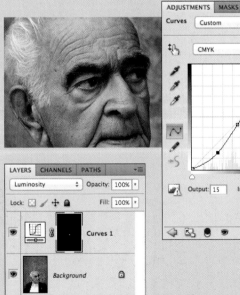

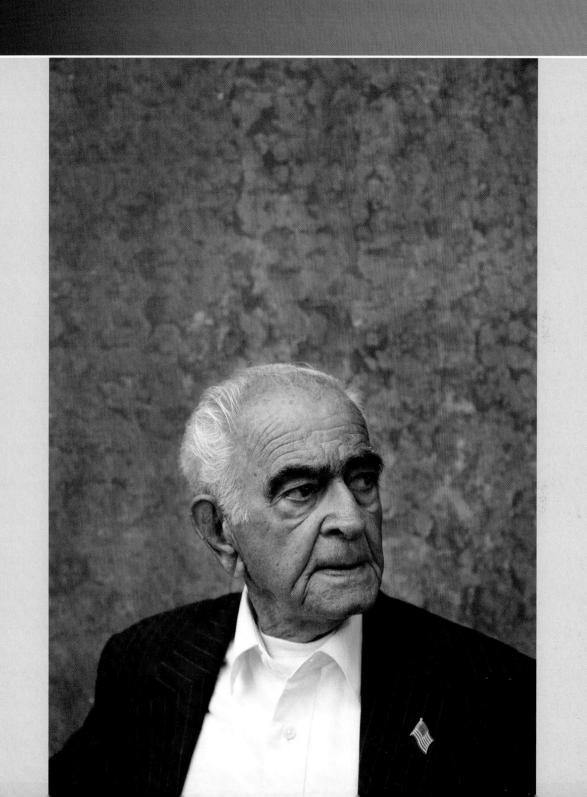

Making Images Pop

I like images that *pop*, by which I mean they possess a good amount of contrast and vibrancy. Most images produced by a digital camera are flat, or at least flatter than I prefer. So when I bring my images into Photoshop for editing, I'm trying to work them toward what I've imagined in my head. This is the case whether the image is color or black-and-white. In fact, the process I often follow for enhancing my color images benefits me when the images are converted over to black-and-white.

1 Preparing the Raw File

I brought the image into the raw converter, where I adjusted for brightest, contrast, sharpness, and white balance. White balance was a particular issue because this scene was illuminated by two different light sources (tungsten and fluorescent), making for a white balance challenge. However, I made whatever adjustment I could in the Adobe Raw Converter (ARC) to optimize the image before launching Photoshop.

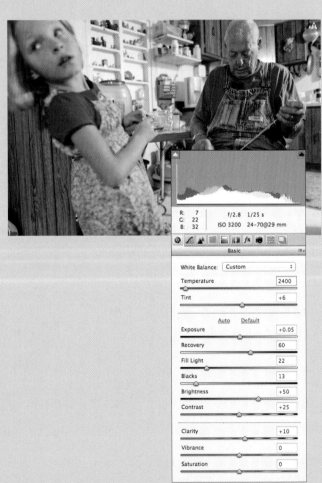

❷ The Levels Adjustment

I created a Levels adjustment layer to establish black and white points. I moved the black slider a little more than usual because I wanted deep blacks. I also wanted the background to appear darker than my subject, so I darkened the overall image. I then created a layer mask and used the Brush tool, with an opacity of 100%, to paint out the effect on the subject and make the foreground color black. Finally, I used a smaller brush at a lesser opacity along the edges of the subject until I completely brushed out the effect.

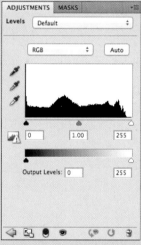

3 **Correcting for Mixed Lighting**

Because I had to work with mixed lighting, I set my white balance to favor the skin tones in the Adobe Raw Converter (ARC), but the kitchen still retained a green color cast from the fluorescent lights. To eliminate this, I created a color balance adjustment layer. With the midtones option selected, I moved the magenta slider to reduce the presence of green and added more magenta to achieve a more natural look to the background. I then copied the layer mask from the previous layer to isolate the color adjustment on the background. To do this, I simply clicked on the layer mask while holding the option key and dragged it over the new layer.

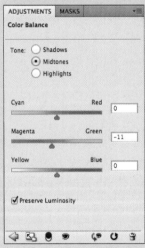

❹ Burning

To emphasize the man tying the shoelaces of his granddaughter's shoe, I knew that I wanted to darken certain areas of the frame, including some of the background, part of her dress, and her right arm. For this, I created a Burn layer by clicking on the New Layer icon at the bottom of the layers palette while holding down the Option/Alt key. I then went to the Mode option and selected Soft Light. I then clicked on the check box for Fill with Soft-light-neutral color (50% gray). Next, I chose the Brush tool, making black my foreground color and, with an opacity of about 15%, painted in those areas that I wanted to darken. I kept the opacity low to ensure that I got a subtle result that didn't look heavy-handed.

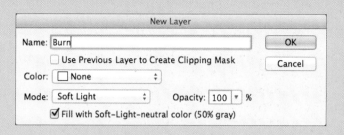

❺ Dodging

I now wanted to selectively brighten certain areas of the frame, so I created a Dodge layer by clicking on the New Layer icon at the bottom of the layers palette while holding down the Option/Alt key. I then went to the Mode option and selected Soft Light and clicked on the check box for "Fill with Soft-light-neutral color (50% gray). With opacity set for 15% and the foreground color set for white, I brightened his face and hands, the shoe, and even the length of the shoestring. By brightening these elements, I helped to draw greater attention to them and guide the viewer's eye.

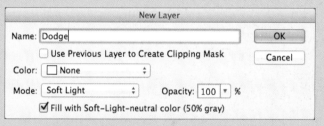

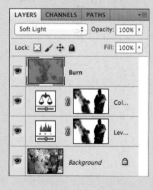

6 **Boosting Contrast**

I liked the image much better now, but I began to
think that the wash of color within the scene was
distracting. The gesture of the grandfather's hands
tying the shoe and the expression on the girl's face
were what this image was really about, but the color
seemed to be a distraction. So, I knew I wanted a
black-and-white. But before I converted the image
to monochrome, I boosted the contrast using a
simple Curves adjustment, limiting the changes to
the shadows and the midtones. Though I could have
done this after I converted the image to black-and-
white, I find that I don't go too far over the top
with contrast when I am evaluating the image as a
color image.

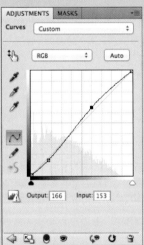
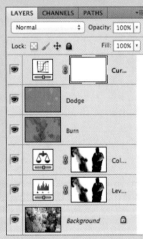

❼ Black-and-White Conversion

I created a Black-and-White Adjustment layer and settled for the Darker preset. However, it made everything equally darker and I lost some of the brightness that I had worked so hard for with my dodging layer. So, while I like the overall black-and-white look, I slowly tweaked the image using the color sliders for the reds and yellows, which brightened up areas of the skin. I toned down the magenta to darken the sleeve of the girl's shirt.

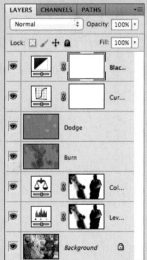

Conclusion

I found that this image worked appreciably better as a black-and-white than it did as a color image. So I was pretty pleased with the look. The final image conveys the moment as well as an important sense of place. Though the work I did for the color image made it stronger, it's the black-and-white version that really expresses what I thought and felt when I made the photograph.

Artist Biographies

Erik Almas

Erik Almas was born in Trondheim, Norway, and moved to San Francisco to study photography at the Academy of Art at the age of 22. He graduated in 1999 with the distinction of "Best Portfolio" in that year's Spring Show. In 2004, the Academy awarded him an Honorary Degree of Outstanding Alumnus. He has since produced advertising campaigns for such clients as Toyota, Hyatt, Puma, Pfizer, Microsoft, Nike, and Spanish Tourism. Erik's work has been featured in *Communication Arts—Photo Annual, Photo District News Photo Annual, American Photography*, and on the cover of *Graphis Photo Annual 2010*. He has been recognized twice by Luerzer's Archive as one of the 200 Best Advertising photographers worldwide. He now resides in San Francisco, which he considers a great place to call home. To see more, visit www.erikalmas.com.

Miss Aniela

Natalie "Miss Aniela" Dybisz was born in 1986 in Leeds, England, and studied English & Media at the University of Sussex. Her career as an artist began whilst still at University, and shortly following, she was invited to speak in the United States for Microsoft and offered solo shows in London and Madrid. She is now a fine art and commercial photographer based in London. Her work has been exhibited in Europe and the United States, with representation in Madrid, Los Angeles, and San Diego, and six solo exhibitions to date. Her work has been featured in *NY Arts Magazine, Fahrenheit Mexico, El Pais, ALARM Chicago, PH Magazine, Vogue Italia, American Photo*, and on the BBC. Miss Aniela's first book, *Self-Portrait Photography*, was published in the United Kingdom and United States in 2011; her second book, *Creative Portrait Photography*, was published in the spring of 2012. She is currently working on a semi-commercial series called "Surreal Fashion" and a fine art environmental series "Ecology." Miss Aniela continues to give talks, and is invited to judge photography competitions. She has also self-branded her own workshop-style event, the "Fashion Shoot Experience," in London and New York. To see more, visit www.missaniela.com.

Adam Baron

Adam Baron is a digital artist and photographer who lives in Tamarac, Florida, with his wife, Sharon, and their two children, Max and Brooke, all of whom have appeared in his work. Initially, Adam was drawn into photography upon discovering the magic of HDR (high dynamic range) photography. Pictures that he knew to be photos yet also seemed illustrated fascinated him. From there, he progressed at learning to edit his pictures and, ultimately, the compositing and manipulation of images to make more complex creations. When he is not taking pictures or editing them, Adam is at his day job masquerading as an attorney. To learn more, please visit www.adambaronphoto.com.

Richard Baxter

My interest in all things visual began at the age of 3, manifesting in an intense love of drawing that has evolved into the painter, photographer, and digital artist that I am today. I first used photography as a teenager to explore and capture material for my paintings. I then embraced the power of Photoshop to compose, enhance, and change images. As a figurative painter for 30 years, a digital artist for 20, and a professional photographer for the past seven years, my skills in the various mediums are now crossing over and enhancing the other areas, helping me create more interesting and refined images. After refining these skills in photography and digital art, they have in turn increased my visual acuity in painting. I am now working with animation and finding the many years of painting, photography, and digital art all come together in the one medium perfectly. To learn more, visit www.studiobaxter.com.

Jaclyn Corrado

Jaclyn Corrado was born and raised in Northern New Jersey. She is currently studying for a Bachelor of Arts in photography at the School of Visual Arts in New York City. Jaclyn began her career in her junior year of high school, and has since received honorable mentions for her work through Scholastic Art and Writing and the National Congressional Art Competition. In September 2012, Jaclyn had her first gallery show at the School of Visual Arts. Her series focuses on representation and the experimental development and process of analog photography. By emphasizing the framing of the photographs themselves, Jaclyn allows viewers to step back and appreciate the process and the craftsmanship that goes into her photos. Jaclyn intends to pursue a career in fashion photography. To learn more, visit www.jaclyncorrado.tumblr.com.

Alexander Corvus

Alexander Corvus was born and educated in Moscow, where he currently resides. In 2004, he got his first film camera and, since then, photography has helped him to create his own visual world. His work has been featured in group and solo exhibitions in Russia and Europe. His photography was the subject of solo shows in Moscow in 2012 and in Saint Petersburg in 2009. His work was exhibited in the Trierenberg Super Circuit in Linz, Vienna, and in the PhotoPodium exhibition in Moscow, both in 2011. In 2009, he participated in the World Photo 2008 exhibition in Ufa. To see more of his work, visit www.alexandercorvus.com.

Star Foreman

Named one of the top 200 photographers in the 2012/2013 edition by Luerzer's Archive, Star Foreman is a fine art, editorial, and fashion photographer in Los Angeles. A contributing photographer for the *LA* and *OC Weekly* magazines, Star's work has also graced the cover of the *Village Voice* and *Pasadena Magazine*, and has been featured in *Rue Magazine, Los Angeles Confidential, Fierce Magazine, Latino Leaders*, and *INStyle Australia*. Star received an honorable mention from the IPA awards (a division of the Lucies) in 2012 for her photo series of Dita Von Teese and was nominated in 2011 for a Los Angeles Press Club Award for her images of Flying Lotus. Two of her pieces are part of the permanent collection at the Riverside Art Museum. Star holds a Bachelor of Arts in photography from the Art Center College of Design in Pasadena, Calif. To learn more, visit www.starforeman.com.

Joel Grimes

Joel Grimes is a professional commercial photographer with more than 30 years of experience. His assignments have taken him to over 50 countries and to every state in the country. In 1992, he produced his first coffee table book, *Navajo, Portrait of a Nation*, which resulted in many accolades, magazine and newspaper articles, and an 18-month exhibition at the Smithsonian American History museum. After two years, 90,000 miles, and close to $100,000, he estimated his work had reached about a million viewers, exposure only 1 percent of all the photographers might have achieved at that time. He is now a passionate proponent of the digital age, which has informed his unique look and the way he shares photography with others. "We are in the greatest age of photography since its conception and, in the end, it has everything to do with our desires as human beings to create." Joel currently resides in Pasadena, Calif., with his wife and two of their sons. To learn more, please go to www.joelgrimes.com.

Valp Maciej Hajnrich

Valp Maciej Hajnrich is a graphic illusionist, art director, and illustrator based in Katowice, Poland. What began as a hobby 15 years ago has grown into a fulfilling career. The self-taught artist takes his inspiration from the visuals in the world around him—from static to motion, ancient to contemporary—and uses a combination of photography manipulation and hand-drawn effects to make his ideas a reality. His work has received considerable recognition, and has been featured in *Digital Arts*, *Advanced Photoshop Magazine*, *Practical Photoshop*, *Los Logos*, *Aktivist*, *Wizz* in-flight magazine, and many other publications. In his spare time, Valp works on personal creative projects, experimenting with style and technique. He is also a member of Keystone Design Union and Depthcore digital arts community. To learn more, visit www.valpnow.com.

Maki Kawakita

Maki Kawakita creates edgy, contemporary images renowned for their bold performance elements and thought-provoking composition. Kawakita's global photography reflects a diverse blend of the Japanese, American, and European cultures that have influenced and inspired her. Her work has taken her from the bustling streets of Manhattan and Tokyo to Milan and the remote landscapes of Tasmania, Turkey, and Kuwait. Kawakita's work has been featured in publications like *Time*, *Marie Claire* and *Vibe*, and she has shot advertising campaigns for Coors Light, Levi Strauss & Co., Virgin Records, Warner Music, and Smirnoff. She also has photographed such celebrities as Beyoncé, Alicia Keys, Paris Hilton, and Arianna Huffington. Recent shows and accolades include a 2009 exhibition at AFAD Gallery in Turkey; a 2008 exhibition at NMM Gallery in Milan, Italy; a 2008 award for portraiture from the Prix de la Photographie in Paris; and selection in 2007 by Commercial Photography as one of the best 100 photographers of Japan. To learn more, visit www.makiphoto.com.

Jim Kazanjian

Jim Kazanjian earned a Bachelor of Fine Arts from the Kansas City Art Institute (Mo.), in 1990 and a Master of Fine Arts from the Art Center College of Design in Pasadena, Calif., in 1992. As a commercial CGI artist in TV and game production, he creates compositions by sifting through thousands of images before finding a few dozen that can be compiled to create something new. His surreal landscapes offer phantasmagoric visions of a where-is-this world, defined by impossibly complex architecture and M.C. Escheresque black-and-white graphics. Inspired by the imaginary realms of cult author H.P. Lovecraft—whose wild, cosmic short stories set the mold for much of the 20th century's best science fiction—Kazanjian's aim is to redress the "misunderstanding that photography has a kind of built-in objectivity." To see more, please visit www.kazanjian.net.

Riley Kern

Riley Kern is a portrait photographer in Orange County, Calif., and Los Angeles. She has a Bachelor of Fine Arts in photography and imaging from The Art Center College of Design, in Pasadena, Ca. Prior to earning that degree, Riley attended The Orange Coast College School of Photography. Her work has most recently been featured on the covers and interiors of *LA and OC Weekly* magazines. Her work has also been featured in *Slake, Deadbeat, Pistol,* and *Evolved*, and has had covers and features in *Tattoo Society* and *MMA Business*. Most recently, the city of Lancaster commissioned her to shoot its 12-month Pin-Up calendar, titled "Support Our Troops." She also shot the cover of the 2012 "Pin-Ups for Pit Bulls" calendar. The British television station Sky hired her to shoot stills for its show "A Year to Save My Life," and she has photographed images for an upcoming book about the artist Shag. Riley has taught workshops for Canon Camera, LADiG, and Belmont High School of the Arts. To see more, visit www.rileykernstudio.com.

Marcos López

Marcos López was born in Santa Fe, Argentina, in 1958 and started practicing photography in 1978. After moving to Buenos Aires in 1982, he immersed himself in traditional black-and-white photography. In the 90s, he began to experiment with color, which led to him developing his Pop series of imagery. His latest series, which includes "Surrealism Criollo," are characterized by staging, where he plays the role of theater director, taking influences from film, painting, and classical documentary photography. His photographs are part of the collections of the National Art Museum and the Reina Sofia Contemporary Art Museum of Castilla y Leon in Spain, the Daros-Latinamerica Foundation in Switzerland, and other public, and private collections. To learn more, visit www.marcoslopez.com.

Holger Maass

Holger Maass, born in 1968, worked as a photojournalist before segueing into fashion and art photography. His photographic stories from China, Thailand, North Korea, Brasil, Russia, and the USA are published in international magazines and newspapers. His current work is published in international art and fashion magazines and appears in art exhibitions in Heidelberg and Munich, Germany; Vienna, Austria; Zurich, Switzerland; Krakow and Warsaw, Poland; and St. Petersburg and Novosibirsk, Russia. Holger is also an adjudicator for international photography competitions. In April 2007, Nikon Corp. invited him to Tokyo as one of the judges for the Nikon Photo Contest International (NPCI). To learn more about Maass, visit www.studio-maass.de.

Stephen Marc

Stephen Marc is a professor of art in the Herberger School of Art at Arizona State University. Marc is in his 35th year of teaching, with 15 years at ASU and 20 years at Columbia College Chicago. Marc was raised in Chicago, and Champaign-Urbana, Ill., was his home away from home. He received his Master of Fine Arts from Tyler School of Art, Temple University in Philadelphia, Penn., and his Bachelor of Arts from Pomona College in Claremont, Calif. He has published three books of his work: *Urban Notions* (1983), where he explored three black communities in Illinois; *The Black Trans-Atlantic Experience: Street Life and Culture in Ghana, Jamaica, England and the United States* (1992); and *Passage on the Underground Railroad* (2009). Marc's current work includes investigations of the Civil Rights and Black Power Movements, Blacks in the West, the relocation of Black Americana imagery, and other aspects of American history with an emphasis on black culture. To learn more, visit www.charlesguice.com/marc.html.

Ibarionex Perello

Ibarionex Perello is a photographer, writer, and educator, and he is the curator of this book. Read more about him on the About the Curator page.

Walter Plotnick

Walter Plotnick is a photo-based artist who lives and works in the Philadelphia area. He received his Master of Fine Arts from University of the Arts and a Bachelor of Fine Arts from Tyler School of Art, Temple University. Walter is an instructor in the Fine Arts Department at Penn State Abington, as well as Montgomery County Community College. His work has been featured in museums, galleries, and exhibitions in Philadelphia, New York, Los Angeles, Germany, Turkey, and Vienna, and he has been the recipient of many awards and grants. To learn more, visit www.walterplotnick.com.

James Porto

James Porto was born in 1960 and raised in Saudi Arabia by an Italian-American father and a Belgian mother. At age 11, he fell in love with photography and, as a teen, documented the desert community of the Saudi Aramco Oil Company. He also discovered a passion in experimental printing. After earning a Bachelor of Science in Professional Photography from Rochester Institute of Technology in 1982, he moved to New York City, where he established a studio on Franklin Street in 1985. A pioneer in multi-image composition techniques, his surrealist aesthetic became popular in campaigns for Absolut, Adidas, AT&T, Blue Man Group, Showtime, Sony, and others. In 1992, he received a fellowship from The New York Foundation for the Arts and began experimenting with emerging digital technologies to further the potential of in-camera and darkroom composite practices. His work has been featured in *American Photo, Photo Italia, The New York Times Magazine, Rolling Stone, Sports Illustrated Swimsuit, New York Magazine, Time, Wired,* and more. For more than 25 years, Mr. Porto has created radically progressive imagery from his Manhattan studio that blurs the accepted line of demarcation between art and commerce. To learn more, visit www.jamesporto.com.

Gediminas Pranckivičius

Gediminas Pranckivičius was born in Lithuania in 1982, where he attended the Vilnius Academy of Fine Arts, specializing in frescoes. After five years as a graphic designer at Cinema Theater, he became a freelance illustrator and concept artist. Since then, he has earned many awards for his work, including 1st place in the CGSociety and NVidia NVArt 4 Surreal Competition. His work has been published in *EXPOSE 10, Digital Art Masters: Volume 6, Digital Painting Techniques: Volume 2, 2D Artist Magazine, Prime—The Definitive Digital Art Collection,* and similar publications. To learn more, visit www.gedomenas.com.

Martine Roch

Martine Roch was in midlife, living in Dijon, France, when she started getting serious about photography. It was 2004, and she had been diagnosed with breast cancer. She dove into photography and Photoshop to take her mind off the disease. She became passionate about her new art form and learned quickly. One day, while looking at a Daguerreotype of a 19th-century lady that she had scanned into Photoshop, Roch looked down at her dog, a golden Labrador Retriever named Boudi. Suddenly, something clicked in her head. "Let's try to dress you as a lady," she said aloud. A career was born. Roch created dozens of these whimsical hybrids, then started posting them on the social networking site Flickr, where they became an immediate Internet sensation. Soon, a French publisher asked if she would license her photos for reproduction on notebooks and postcards, followed quickly by a request from a German publisher. Today, her notebooks and postcards are sold worldwide. People don't give animals enough credit for being intelligent, Roch believes. "They think animals are like objects," Roch says, "but they have feelings and emotions. They have their own way of thinking and reacting to what they see and feel." To see more, visit www.martineroch-studio.com.

Christopher Schneberger

Christopher Schneberger is an artist/photographer in Chicago whose work has been exhibited nationally and internationally. Recent exhibitions include the Annenberg Space for Photography in Los Angeles; Dorsky Projects in New York; Geocarto International in Hong Kong; the 3D Center for Art and Photography in Portland, Ore.; and Printworks Gallery in Chicago, where he is represented. Christopher has twice been the recipient of an Illinois Arts Council individual artist grant. He is an Adjunct Professor at Columbia College Chicago, and is the Department Head for Digital Arts and Photography at the Lillstreet Art Center. He is a founding member of Perspective Gallery, a nonprofit gallery of photography in Evanston, Ill., where he also serves on the Board of Directors. Christopher received his Bachelor of Fine Arts degree from the University of Florida, where he studied with Evon Streetman and Jerry Uelsmann, and earned his Master of Fine Arts degree from Indiana University, where he studied with Jeffrey Wolin. He is also a drummer playing in several bands in the Chicago music scene. He was born and raised in Miami, Florida. To learn more, visit www.christopherschneberger.com.

Brooke Shaden

Brooke Shaden was born in March 1987 in Lancaster, Pa. She was photographically reborn in December 2008 after graduating from Temple University with degrees in film and English. Brooke began creating self-portraits for ease and to have full control over the images, but she has since grown into a self-portrait artist. In her self-portraits, Brooke attempts to place herself within worlds she wishes we could live in, where secrets float out in the open, where the impossible becomes possible. By using painters' techniques as well as the square format, traditional photographic properties are replaced by otherworldly elements. Brooke's photography questions the definition of what it means to be alive. She now resides in Los Angeles, Calif., with her husband and two cats. To see more, visit www.brookeshaden.com.

Scott Stulberg

Scott Stulberg has been enamored by photography since he was 10 years old when his father gave him a camera. His images are currently represented by Corbis, Getty Images, and many others. Scott has taught Photography and Photoshop for many years at different schools and, in 2011, won Outstanding Instructor of the Year at UCLA Extension. And though he hasn't shot film in years, Scott realizes that photography is more than talking about pixels: It is about vision, ideas, and the willingness to allow your imagination to soar. Scott and his fiancé, Holly, currently reside in Sedona, Arizona, where they moved in late 2011. Please visit www.asa100.com to learn more.

Tony Sweet

After successful careers as a jazz musician, educator, and professional magician, Tony settled on photography as his chosen means for personal expression. Beginning as a film photographer, he reluctantly moved to the digital age. Probably the last of his peers to "go digital," Tony has become facile in imaging software, specializing in plug-ins. As a charter Nik Team member, Tony teaches and lectures throughout the United States and Canada on the creative use of plug-ins. Tony and Susan Milestone conduct Visual Artistry photography location workshops in the United States, Canada, and Iceland. His photography is published worldwide in every medium and is represented by Getty Images. His iPhone Photography is represented by Aurora Photos. Nikon, Nik Software, Singh Ray, Alien Skin, Lens Baby, and others have also used Tony's images for national campaigns. He is the author of five books on the art of photography: *Fine Art Nature Photography, Fine Art Flower Photography, Fine Art Nature Photography: Water, Ice Fog, Fine Art digital Photography,* and *HDR Photography.* To learn more, visit www.tonysweet.com.

Tim Tadder

Tim Tadder is also a visual communicator who produces award-winning campaigns for top consumer brands, including Adidas, Budweiser, Coke Zero, Craftsman, Gatorade, and more. He creates highly stylized images that draw viewers into a decisive moment. Tim has always been active in sports, exploration, and adventure and believes that being familiar with shooting live action makes it easier to re-create the look for advertising shoots. Tim grew up in Baltimore, Md., the son of a sports photographer, and as a teen spent hours photographing his friends' skateboarding exploits. But he didn't pick up the camera seriously until he was an adult. Tim lives in Southern California with his wife and two daughters and feels lucky to be able to make a living doing something that he really loves in the beach town of Encinitas. To learn more, visit www.timtadder.com.

Sean Teegarden

Sean Teegarden is a Los Angeles-based freelance photographer, specializing in portraiture, still life, and commercial advertising. He also retouches for several high-end clients, and consults for Adobe Systems on digital imaging. His images have been highlighted for such prestigious competitions as the Adobe Design Achievement Awards, *Photo District News'* Pix Digital Imaging Award, and Apple's Insomnia Photo Festival. A graduate of Art Center College of Design in Pasadena, Calif., Sean is deeply influenced by his roots as a native Angelino, his time in the scouting program, and his love of midcentury Americana. To learn more, visit www.seanteegarden.com.

Nick Vedros

At the age of 13, Nick Vedros was inspired to become a photographer after seeing his Uncle Mike's black-and-white photographs on the family kitchen table. Upon graduating from the University of Missouri with a degree in photojournalism in 1976, he found his true passion in the world of commercial photography. In the hands of a photographer driven to make every shot his best, it is simple to understand why Nick's work garners top honors from the Addys, The Effies, Archive International, *Communication Arts*, N.A.M.A., the Top 200 Advertising Photographers, and the Canon Explorer of Light Program. His award-winning methodology attracts blue chip clients like Apple, Bayer, Capital One, Coca-Cola, DuPont, IBM, Kodak, Microsoft, Sony, and Sprint. For more information, see www.vedros.com.

William George Wadman

William George Wadman is an American portrait photographer living in New York City. His editorial portrait work has been seen on the covers and pages of major magazines throughout the world. In 2007, Bill completed a yearlong portrait project that involved posting a new image every day. His 365portraits.com won praise from *USA Today*, *The Times of London*, *Playboy*, and was chosen as *Yahoo! Site of the Day*. The Drabbles series of cinematic portraits garnered a solo show at New York's SoHo Photo Gallery in 2010 and inclusion in a juried exhibit at the John B. Aird Gallery in Toronto in May 2012. Inspired by a number of professional dancers, Bill completed his long-exposure series, "Motion," in 2009. The images have been featured in numerous magazines, including *Eloquence*, *Popular Photography*, and *PhotoYou*. Bill has been a contributor to *TIME*, *Business Week*, *Improper Bostonian*, *POZ*, *Popular Photography*, *The New York Times*, *La Monde*, *Eloquence*, *Der Spiegel*, *Wharton Magazine*, *The Times of London*, *USA Today*, *The University of Chicago Magazine*, *Fast Company*, and *WIRED.com*. He can't stand coffee but does drink Coke out of a 500 mL beaker. Opinionated and voraciously autodidactic, Bill loves meeting his subjects almost as much as shooting them. To learn more, visit www.billwadman.com.

Dean West

Dean West has a highly conceptual and thought-provoking style of contemporary portraiture, in which he transforms stick figure sketches into intricate composited photographs with detail and clarity. Born in small-town Australia in 1983, Dean's passion for photography began in high school and blossomed at the Queensland College of Art, Griffith University, Brisbane. There, he majored in visual culture and advertising and earned a Bachelor of Photography in 2007. His body of work has been featured in top photography magazines, art galleries, and received numerous international awards. Australia's *Capture Magazine* recognized Dean as one of the world's best emerging photographers and, in 2008, he won Saatchi & Saatchi's Advertising Photographer of the Year at the International Aperture Awards. Dean's body of work is now being collected by a growing number of sophisticated art collectors in Australia, Italy, and Canada. To see more, visit www.deanwest.com.

Sarah Wilmer and Mike Schultz

Sarah Wilmer and Mike Schultz are longtime friends who indulge in cat appreciation. They met on a glacier in Tierra del Fuego and have made artwork together ever since—even once on an active volcano! Sarah is a Brooklyn-based photographer whose recent projects include photographing wild children on a deserted island, photo hunting through the buildings and streets of New York City, making sense of travel imagery, and capturing creatures in nature. Mike is an oil painter currently based in Portland, Ore. Recently, he lived on the Thai-Burma border, where he helped to establish the Puzzlebox Art Studio in Mae Sot, Thailand, a functional arts and crafts production studio that focuses on apprenticing migrant youth from Burma. Visit www.sarahwilmer.com to learn more.

About the Curator

Ibarionex Perello

Like many others of my generation, I was seduced by photography the moment I saw an image magically appear on a blank piece of paper floating in a developing tray. In the many decades since, the practice of photography has been irrevocably connected with that emotional wave of discovery and possibility.

Though the age of digital has changed the process of capturing and outputting an image, the power of a photograph to reveal the world in a unique and different way has not.

In my role as an editor, writer, and producer, I am lucky enough to discover how other photographers see and explore the world. And even better yet, with my podcast, The Candid Frame (www.thecandidframe.com), I have the opportunity to sit down and converse with these visionaries to gain a greater understanding of what drives them to create their images and why.

The show and this book provide insights into my own process and my photography in a way that's invaluable. So, when I walk out the door with the camera slung over my shoulder, I have the wealth of experience of the thousands of photographers whose lives and art have touched my creative life.

As I continue to chase after my own photographic pursuits, I am constantly encouraged by the wealth of talent and endless imagination of those who are similarly following their passion to make the next photograph their best.